The
Connell Guide
to
Virginia Woolf's

Mrs Dalloway

by
John Sutherland and Susanna Hislop

Contents

NOTES

Introduction

It is hard to find anyone nowadays who will dare venture a bad word on *Mrs Dalloway*: its status as major literature, a pioneer feminist text and a brilliantly experimental work, is wholly secure. Woolf is, with Jane Austen, the leading woman novelist in English Literature, and this novel is one of the peaks of her literary achievement. In short, *Mrs Dalloway* is a "classic".

At the time of its publication, however, opinions were more mixed than ours. It was hard in the mid-1920s to come to terms with what, for many, seemed a vexatiously new-fangled work. The reading public was not yet ready for the challenge of what came to be called "stream of consciousness" narrative, or the inner richness of a novel whose main event, a superficial reading might suggest, is an upper-class Conservative politician's wife's purchase of flowers for a summer party. This, recall, in the immediate aftermath of a conflict, the First World War, which had shaken the whole of Europe to its foundations.

It was without doubt an intellectual and well-ordered novel, granted P.C. Kennedy in his contemporary review – but "there are no people". By which he meant characters a reader like himself could easily identify with. Virginia Woolf's arch-rival, Arnold Bennett, about whom she would write scathingly (and amusingly), snorted angrily that he couldn't finish the damn thing because there was no logical "construction". Where was Woolf's story going? Was there a story? For Bennett, *Mrs Dalloway* was a novel without "plot": for Kennedy it was a novel without "characters" – those two basic ingredients of the realist novel from whose conventions Woolf's work of fiction so willfully and skillfully departs.

Even Woolf's friend, and fellow Bloomsbury Group stalwart, E. M. Forster, expressed private doubts about her ability to create "rounded", or fully living, characters of the kind he so relished and created in novels like *Howards End*. But he did praise the visual qualities of *Mrs Dalloway*: "How beautifully she sees!", as he put it. It is not the highest of literary praise. In the Cambridge critic F.R. Leavis's conservative literary journal, *Scrutiny* (founded in 1932), blue-stocking Muriel Bradbrook attacked *Mrs Dalloway* head on, pointing contemptuously at its "astonishingly ingenuous" heroine who was "preserved in a kind of intellectual vacuum". No plot, no character, no serious ideas. The "Scrutineers" waged ceaseless war against the "Bloomsberries", who they (wrongly) thought to be effete dilettantes. For the disciples of Leavis the great novelist, the epitome of the "Great Tradition" in English fiction, was D. H. Lawrence – a novelist of very pronounced ideas indeed who, it was felt in Cambridge, got to grips with life. Lawrence himself had little time for

Virginia Woolf. Reading novels like *Mrs Dalloway*, he said, was like being shaken up in a feather mattress until you felt like a feather yourself. Neatly put – but grossly unfair.

Woolf was, Lawrence might well have said, "narrow-gutted" – the offensive term he applied to Jane Austen. And upper-class with it. Woolf wrote a famous polemic, *A Room of One's Own*, demanding domestic space and independence for women like herself to be fully creative. But Woolf always had servants to clean her domestic space (and turn her mattresses) in the fine houses she was brought up in and lived in all her life.

Her life was certainly materially comfortable but anything but comfortable temperamentally. Before, during, and after writing *Mrs Dalloway* Woolf teetered on the edge of mental breakdown, and more than once fell into its awful depths. She could as readily have identified with Charlotte Brontë's madwoman in the attic as sensible little Jane Eyre. On the edge of the main plot of *Mrs Dalloway*, and its heroine's outwardly serene existence, Woolf places Septimus Smith – a shell-shocked survivor of the Great War who finds peacetime too terrible to continue living in.

These topics and many others, covered in the pages that follow, need to be taken on board, assessed, and given their proper weight. *Mrs Dalloway* is a novel which, in a sense, one must learn – from its pages themselves – how profitably to appreciate. It is also a novel which provokes thought about the fraught nature of genius, literary modernism, the ambiguous place of women in English society and literature, the infinite complexities of sexual relationships, and even the worthwhileness of life itself. The last was a burning issue for Virginia Woolf. It is one of the inestimable losses to English literature that she decided, in April 1941, that life was, after all, not worth living and killed herself, aged 59 (Mrs Dalloway is 52). Was it a rational act, or an act of madness? Biography is divided on the subject.

The reader must start from the position that *Mrs Dalloway* is an unusually complex work of literature. The aim of what follows is to outline and, as best one can, define that complexity and to suggest ways in which, with reading and re-reading, one can win through it for one of the most rewarding experiences English fiction has to offer.

A summary of the plot

It is not an easy novel to read, but *Mrs Dalloway* is the easiest of novels to summarise. "A day in the life of a middle-aged upper class woman planning her party" is how the *Oxford Companion to Twentieth-Century Literature* encapsulates it. The day is 13th June, 1923 by the best guess we can make. The "upper class woman" is Clarissa

Dalloway, the wife of a middle-ranking Conservative politician who has never quite made it into the Cabinet.

She is recovering from a serious illness and depression, for which she has been treated by eminent Harley Street physicians and therapists.

The long prelude to the party is Clarissa's

THE ORIGINS OF MRS DALLOWAY

Richard and Clarissa Dalloway first appeared in Woolf's first novel, *The Voyage Out* (1915). In their first incarnation, as Elaine Showalter notes, they are slightly comic figures. Clarissa is "a tall slight woman, her body wrapped in furs, her face in veils", with artistic tastes but no brains to speak of. Richard is a Tory MP with conventional opinions on everything. He vows at one point that he will be in his grave before a woman is ever allowed to vote in England.

Then, in August 1922, Woolf wrote the short story "Mrs Dalloway in Bond Street", believing it might serve as the first chapter of a novel. She quickly began to wonder about a sequel. "Shall I write the next chapter of Mrs D. – if she is to have a next chapter; & shall it be The Prime Minister?"

In this first phase, the novel made much of the contrast between Clarissa, the society hostess, and the Prime Minister, who drives through London and will come to her party. In this version, says Showalter, Clarissa "buying gloves in Bond Street, is the epitome of the leisured lady of the ruling-class for whom the Empire exists. The Prime Minister is the target for all morning walk through the West End of London to collect the flowers for the party she and her husband are throwing that evening. When she returns from buying the blooms she finds she has a visitor – Peter Walsh. Thirty years earlier they had been on the brink of marriage, in an affair which reached its emotional climax at a country

---

the feelings of resentment and hopelessness felt by the excluded and deprived man in the street."

Gradually, during late 1922 and early 1923, Woolf's ideas evolved. Septimus became a character then, in May 1923, she came up with the idea of an old suitor for Clarissa: Peter Walsh. "There shd. now be a long talk between Mrs D. & some old buck." Struggling with the problem of making her characters more than two-dimensional and getting the element of time into the book through the characters' memories, she hit on the solution at the end of August:

> My discovery: how I dig out beautiful caves behind my characters; I think that gives exactly what I want; humanity, humour, depth.

Throughout the novel's composition, Woolf was trying out new approaches and possibilities. How should she pull it all together with images and allusions? Art helped, says Showalter. "Cubist paintings, strange as they looked to the uninitiated eye, had a unity on the canvas that came from the use of colour, and from the boundary of the frame.

In *Mrs Dalloway*, the striking of Big Ben acts as a temporal grid to organise the narrative." Indeed Woolf's working title during most of the writing of the novel was "The Hours", and the continual chiming of clocks keeps us aware of "the passage of time and the measuring out of human lives and seasons" ∎

house, Bourton.

Clarissa declined Peter's proposal and they went their separate ways. He migrated to India, and missed the war. There is a woman in India, Daisy, with whom he may, or may not, have a relationship. His conversation with Clarissa is unsatisfactory and he goes off, disconsolately, to ruminate in Regent's Park, fiddling all the while with the penknife in his pocket. He has, he may feel, fiddled his life away.

The park is also where a World War One veteran, Septimus Smith, is walking with his Italian wife, Lucrezia, a hat maker. Septimus is still suffering from shellshock, and is seriously deranged. The birds, he fantasises, are talking to him – in ancient Greek. (This actually happened to Woolf in one of her breakdowns.) Before the war he was a sensitive, promising poet. During the conflict he had an intense relationship with his officer in the trenches, Evans, who was killed. It haunts him.

Septimus is about to go for a consultation with Clarissa's Harley Street psychiatrist, Sir William Bradshaw. No help is forthcoming. Sir William's advice is platitudinous and useless. Septimus must be moved to an asylum.

The narrative focus shifts to Richard, Clarissa's husband, at lunch with two friends, Hugh Whitbread and Lady Bruton; they talk of grand affairs of state. Richard returns home with a bunch of roses for Clarissa. He senses their relationship has, obscurely, gone wrong. He is right.

The focus moves again to Septimus and Lucrezia at home, waiting for removal to the asylum. In terror, he throws himself out of a window, impaling himself, fatally, on the spiked iron railings below. As the ambulance bell rings Peter, who hears it, goes to Clarissa's party.

Also present at the party is Sally Seton, with whom Clarissa fell in love many years earlier, during her days at Bourton. Once a tomboy, Sally is now dull Lady Rosseter. News of Septimus's death arrives and is gossiped about. Clarissa feels a bond with the dead man – stronger, perhaps, than that for her husband or her near-adult daughter, Elizabeth (on the brink of conversion to evangelical Christianity). The novel ends, inconclusively, after the party.

What is *Mrs Dalloway* about?

Virginia Woolf, like her predecessors Jane Austen and George Eliot, "chose on the whole to describe women less gifted, intellectually less audacious, more conventional than herself". Margaret Drabble's shrewd remark certainly applies to the society lady at the centre of Woolf's fourth novel.

Even her creator had doubts about her, wondering if she was "too glittering & tinselly". Many of Woolf's contemporaries, and many critics too, have found her class-bound and slight. At her most interesting, argues the contemporary novelist Paul Bailey, "Mrs Dalloway is a snobbish, vain, repressed lesbian who has dabbled in culture, but for the greater part of the novel she is only a shadow, poetically enshrined".

At the other extreme, Sandra Gilbert and Susan Gubar, leaders of post-1960s feminist revisionism, have hailed Woolf's heroine as "a kind of queen" who "with a divine grace... regenerates the post-war world", though to claim Mrs Dalloway as some kind of feminist heroine requires considerable ingenuity. As Elaine Showalter, another revisionist, notes, Woolf's deliberately banal title, with its emphasis on the heroine's married status, stands in sharp contrast to James Joyce's mythically titled *Ulysses*, which she read shortly before writing *Mrs Dalloway*. Clarissa is neither a priestess nor a goddess – to substitute "a liberated Ms Dalloway for Woolf's ambiguous heroine" is absurd; she is "rather an ordinary woman on an ordinary day. Indeed what is so moving and profound about the book is the way Woolf sees behind people's social masks to their deepest human concerns, without elevating them to the level of myth."

Mrs Dalloway is an anti-heroic novel. Almost

all the characters have failed to live up to their youthful dreams. Clarissa senses her life has been shallow and passionless; her husband's political career has fallen far short of his hopes; the Socialist Peter Walsh has never fulfilled his literary ambitions. The novel's most out-and-out rebel, the "wild, the daring, the romantic" Sally Seton, has ended up married to a bald manufacturer from Manchester, while the intellectual Doris Kilman has become an embittered religious fanatic. Septimus Smith, who dreamed of being a poet, has had his mind and belief in life shattered by the war and feels he can't be loved.

All these figures are haunted by the past, by the shadow of their own past failures and by the tragic aftermath of World War One. We shall never escape our memories, Woolf suggests. They play the central role in shaping our consciousness, in determining our sanity. Indeed the nature of consciousness – and of sanity – is Woolf's main preoccupation in *Mrs Dalloway*. In a diary entry for 14th October 1922, she commented that her work in progress would be "a study of insanity & suicide: the world seen by the sane & the insane side by side – something like that".

"The doors would be taken off their hinges," we are told in the third sentence of the novel, in reference to the preparations for Clarissa's party. It seems like the most incidental of details but the sentence may also prompt us to ask ourselves which characters in the novel are "unhinged". Is Clarissa herself merely eccentric or is she dangerously unbalanced? Before Septimus is even brought into the action, her "acute strangeness" is carefully established:

> *She felt very young; at the same time unspeakably aged. She sliced like a knife through everything; at the same time was outside, looking on. She had a perpetual sense... of being out, out, far out to sea and alone; she always had the feeling that it was very, very dangerous to live even one day.*

She is uncertain what time of year this is, despite it being the day of her party. At one point

THE BLOOMSBURY GROUP

The Bloomsbury Group, of which Virginia Woolf was the leading light, included among its most notable members the novelist E.M. Forster, the art critic Roger Fry, the poet Rupert Brooke, and the most influential economist of the 20th century, Maynard Keynes. The leading propagandist was Lytton Strachey, who proclaimed their founding principle – that they were not, repeat not, Victorians (even though all of them had been born and raised during Victoria's reign).

For the Bloomsbury Group

she says it is "the middle of June"; at another that June is "still untouched... almost whole". She feels "the oddest sense of being herself invisible; unseen; unknown", and when she notices a "salmon on an iceblock" in a Bond Street fishmonger's shop she comments out loud: "That is all... That is all." Is her mind 'going'? As the critic David Bradshaw says, it is a "tad unusual" for someone of Clarissa's age and educational background not to know "what the Equator was", and

in view of her husband's profession, the prolonged and widespread coverage which the Turkish slaughters of Armenians in 1894-96 and 1915 received in the British press, and the way in

---

the "Eminent Victorians", as Strachey sneeringly labelled them in his famous book, existed largely to be mocked and repudiated. But most importantly got out of the way. (The Bloomsberries regarded the First World War as the death throes of Victorianism – though tragic, it made possible a new start in literature and the realm of ideas.) What then did Bloomsbury stand for? Civilisation, they might have answered, or Liberalism. They subscribed to a philosophy which originated with John Stuart Mill and was reformulated by the Cambridge philosopher, G.E. Moore. The essential idea was that you were free to do anything so long as it did not damage, or infringe on the equivalent freedoms of some other person. It's a nice principle, but extremely hard to put into practice. Some would say impossible ∎

which the continuing persecution of Armenians in Turkey was closely monitored in British newspapers between 1915 and the early 1920s, Clarissa's "muddl[ing] Armenians and Turks" is only a little less bizarre than muddling Jews and Nazis would be in the latter half of the following decade.

To Clarissa, her daughter's tutor, Doris Kilman, is nothing less than a threatening incubus, "one of those spectres which one battles in the night; one of those spectres who stand astride us and suck up half our life-blood, dominators and tyrants". Kilman is "Elizabeth's seducer; the woman who had crept in to steal and defile"; Clarissa feels a hatred, a "brutal monster" lurking inside her with "icy claws". The terrible flu epidemic which struck after World War One, killing more Britons than the war had done, did not leave survivors mentally damaged, but the hatred Clarissa feels

especially since her illness, had power to make her feel scraped, hurt in her spine; gave her physical pain, and made all pleasure in beauty, in friendship, in being well, in being loved and making her home delightful, rock, quiver and bend as if indeed there were a monster grubbing at the roots, as if the whole panoply of content were nothing but self love! this hatred!

Virginia Woolf, circa *1930*

Septimus's affliction is expressed in similar terms: both he and Clarissa have suicidal tendencies, with the perilousness of Clarissa's life underlined, perhaps, by her husband's gift of red and white roses, a combination which, while it may be patriotic, has often been seen by the superstitious as an omen of death.

In her introduction to the Modern Library Edition of *Mrs Dalloway* written in 1928, Woolf was explicit: Septimus "is intended to be [Clarissa's] double". "By acquainting the reader with Clarissa's strangeness in advance of Septimus's," says David Bradshaw, "the latter's abnormality is to some extent normalised and the response of the medical establishment made to

THE SKY-WRITING PLANE

The sound of an aeroplane bored ominously into the ears of the crowd. There it was coming over the trees, letting out white smoke from behind, which curled and twisted, actually writing something! making letters in the sky!

Everyone looked up... The plane is advertising something mysterious (though Septimus sees it is a signal from the gods, calling on him to be the messiah). In its final arc, it is compared to Shelley's skylark, "curving up and up, straight up, like something mounting in ecstasy, in pure delight", while "out from behind poured white smoke looping, writing a T, an O, an F".

Gillian Beer describes this passage as erotic and

seem all the more arbitrary and unjust."

In a novel which explores the boundaries of sanity and insanity, other characters behave oddly, too, not least Peter Walsh. He is described as "cranky"; when Clarissa first sees him she notices he has "the same queer look"; she also notices his "extraordinary habit" of playing with his pocket-knife. Some critics have seen the knife as a symbol of virility, or sexual predatoriness, but Bradshaw thinks it "more eloquently represents the knife-edge equilibrium of his mind" and links him with Clarissa who slices "like a knife through everything". To the girl who serves her in the Army and Navy Stores, Doris Kilman also seems "mad", so obsessively does she study the petticoats on

---

playful: "toffs and toffee are indistinguishable, farts in the wake of lark, of sexual rapture". Freud thought that, almost as soon as it was invented, the aeroplane became a symbol of sexual excitement in people's dreams.

Aerial sky-writing was invented by a British aviator, Major Jack Savage, and was first seen in London in August 1922. "If not in every part of the country," said *The Times*, "at least for a hundred miles around London the writing of advertisements in the sky by aircraft has been seen by millions of people." In America, three months later, Captain Cyril Turner, wrote "Hello, USA!" in the sky over Manhattan. By 1923, the *Daily Mail* was regularly using sky-writing as an advertising device. According to Noreen Bronson in *Britain in the Nineteen Twenties*, city workers could see the paper's name "in giant letters of orange and silver" ■

display, and Miss Kilman talks aloud to herself, a habit she shares with Clarissa, Peter and Septimus.

Sir William Bradshaw may think "health is proportion" and "not having a sense of proportion" betokens insanity, but the novel challenges this view, raising the question of whether anyone can really determine precisely where clinical insanity begins and mere idiosyncracy ends.

"Clarissa and Septimus uncannily share what seems a single consciousness, intense and vulnerable, each fearing to be consumed by a fire perpetually about to break forth," says the American critic Harold Bloom. The doubling of the two characters "implies there is only a difference in degree, not in kind, between Clarissa's sensibility and the naked consciousness of 'madness' of Septimus". As Woolf herself puts it,

MADNESS

There is an interesting sideline to this debate on mental derangement at the heart of *Mrs Dalloway*. There is a tradition that it is only in a kind of madness – "furor poeticus", the ancients called it – that reality can be apprehended in its full nature. "If a man could live truly in the present," says Schopenhauer, "he would die of intoxication." Woolf, of course, had had a series of serious breakdowns before writing *Mrs Dalloway*. Horrible as they may have been to experience, they may have contributed to the artistry she achieved in the novel ■

"Clarissa sees the truth, SS sees the insane truth". Through the doubling of her two characters, and the parallels she draws between them, Woolf seeks to show how, for sensitive people, the experience of being alive is not radically different, is in many respects very similar, even among those who may on the surface seem to be poles apart.

What is distinctive about the narrative voice?

Virginia Woolf gave much thought to the question of what a novel should be, writing frequently about the difference between her generation of novelists, including E.M. Forster, D.H. Lawrence and James Joyce, and their Edwardian predecessors, Arnold Bennett, John Galsworthy and H.G. Wells. At the beginning of 1918, early chapters of Joyce's *Ulysses* were sent to the Hogarth Press, which she had founded with her husband, Leonard, in the hope they would publish it. (They didn't.) Virginia Woolf also physically typeset the entire text of her close friend T.S. Eliot's *The Waste Land*.

Like both of these modernist classics, *Mrs Dalloway* is an experiment in narrative form. In a famous essay, "Mr Bennett and Mrs Brown" (1924), Woolf argued that since 1910 all human relations have shifted – those between masters and servants, husbands and wives, parents and children. And when human relations change, there is at the same time a change in religion, conduct, politics, and literature.

Although she claimed the date was "arbitrary", it wasn't really arbitrary: 1910 was the start of the new Georgian era (following Edward VII's death, George V ascended the throne in May); more importantly, it was the year of "Manet and the Post-Impressionists", the controversial exhibition organised by Woolf's friend and Bloomsbury luminary, Roger Fry. This radical display of European art shocked the London bourgeoisie, viewers and critics alike. Art historian Charles Harrison has recorded the way people recoiled at the exhibition's "horror", "madness", "pornography", "anarchy" and "evil". Woolf, though jealous of the art world's celebrity, was thrilled: "is it not possible that some writer will come along and do in words what these men have done in paint?"

In "Mr Bennett and Mrs Brown", she argued that neither human character nor human relationships could be adequately represented by the literary conventions of the Edwardians. "For us," she asserted dramatically, "those conventions are ruin, those tools are death." An "external narrator" and a "symmetrically arranged" narrative did not mirror the fragmented reality of the modern consciousness. Woolf had spotted a "clean, threadbare" old lady on a train. How would the Edwardians have urged a young writer to describe this woman, whom she called "Mrs Brown"? They would have told the writer:

> "Begin by saying that her father kept a shop in Harrogate. Ascertain the rent. Ascertain the wages of shop assistants in the year 1878. Discover what her mother died of. Describe cancer. Describe calico. Describe" – But I cried "Stop! Stop!" And I regret to say that I threw that ugly, that clumsy, that incongruous tool out of the window, for I knew that if I began describing the cancer and the calico, my Mrs Brown, that vision to which I cling though I know no way of imparting it to you, would have been dulled and tarnished for ever.

As her own generation of novelists looked for new ways of capturing character, readers would have to get used to "a season of fragments or failures". But they should be patient: "we are trembling on the verge of one of the great ages of English literature".

Elaine Showalter, one of *Mrs Dalloway*'s most perceptive contemporary critics, finds it tempting to see Mrs Brown as a "poor relation" of Clarissa, and to read this essay as a manifesto for Woolf's own work in progress, "in which external facts are thin upon the ground (for example, we have no idea when or how Clarissa's mother died), and consciousness is everything". It is also interesting, as Showalter notes, that while Woolf

> omits gender from the list of the variables affecting the novelist's point of view – "age, country, and temperament" – she names both her adversaries and her allies as male novelists wielding clumsy and violent tools, while their mutual object is an obscure and enigmatic old woman.

But while Woolf doesn't frame her argument in feminist terms, the clumsiness of the literary conventions she deplores "seem connected to the problem of representing the feminine character", a point which, five years later, in the famous essay, *A Room of One's Own*, she makes herself, arguing that women novelists faced the problem that the language, syntax and value system of the novel was originally created by men, who occupied all the literary spaces.

If, in writing *Mrs Dalloway*, Virginia Woolf was looking for a more sympathetic way of rendering consciousness, in particular female consciousness, she was also grappling with the fact that the very

Opposite: Virginia Woolf with T.S. Eliot. They were close friends for more than 20 years, pioneers of the modernist movement. Eliot said in his obituary of Woolf: "Without Virginia Woolf at the center of it, it would have remained formless or marginal... With the death of Virginia Woolf, a whole pattern of culture is broken."

concept of character and personality was changing for her generation of novelists. The human personality, says Showalter, was coming to be seen not as "one given fixed monolithic entity", but as a "shifting conglomerate of impressions and emotions". Psycholanalysis was "uncovering a multi-layered self, in which dreams, memories, and fantasies were as important as actions and facts". The Woolfs' Hogarth Press published Freud's works – in 1921 – and Woolf developed her own psychological method of explaining memory and repression, which resembled Freud's in many respects.

Like Freud, Woolf believed that early childhood is crucial in shaping our adult identity. *Mrs Dalloway* is full of flashbacks and fragments from

A ROOM OF HER OWN

Virginia Woolf's "room of her own" in London's Richmond (where she and Leonard lived in a large town house), like the couple's second home in rural Sussex, was cleaned and kept tidy and warm by grossly underpaid live-in servants – earning a pittance a year. In her monograph *Mrs Woolf & the Servants: The Hidden Heart of Domestic Service,* Alison Light tells the story of two of the Woolfs' servants, Nellie Boxall and Lottie Hope. Who, one may ask, is (invisibly) doing Mrs Dalloway's washing up and making the beds on that fine day in June? One should not make too much of this, but it is worth bearing in mind ∎

childhood experience. Early on, we learn that Clarissa, when she feels deserted, jealous and excluded, climbs the stairs to her room and thinks of herself as a "child exploring a tower". Later, the reader learns that what Showalter calls "this odd image, with its Freudian hint of the little girl's discovery of sexuality and the phallic" has its origins in Clarissa's childhood:

> *She had gone up into the tower alone and left them blackberrying in the sun. The door had shut, and there among the dust of fallen plaster and the litter of birds' nests how distant the view had looked, and the sounds came thin and chill (once on Leith Hill, she remembered).*

This is a subtle passage in which Woolf doesn't intervene with an explanation but, says Showalter,

> leaves the memory itself to resonate for us, with its echoes of fairy-tale princesses locked in towers, as well as with the more symbolic nuances of a Yeatsian winding tower of age, and of human isolation and loneliness.

Woolf seeks to deepen our understanding of Clarissa through memories and dreams, rather than telling us more directly, as an omniscient narrator might, what her heroine thought and felt. Even the domineering Lady Bruton becomes more sympathetic when we learn that, in her dreams, she is still a bedraggled tomboy jumping the brooks in Devonshire on her pony.

For Woolf, external events matter because of the way they affect our thoughts and condition our inner life. The technique she uses, a development of so-called "free indirect discourse", has often been labelled "stream of consciousness", a phrase first used by the American psychologist William James (brother of the novelist Henry James, who knew Woolf's family well), to describe the flow of conscious and less than conscious experience in the mind. The writers described as using this technique, including Katherine Mansfield – the only writer, Woolf said she really envied – have done so in different ways, though all have shared

STREAM OF CONSCIOUSNESS

Woolf, like Joyce and, before him, Flaubert, wanted to extend what is known as "free indirect discourse" – when the novelist takes on the thought or speech patterns of a particular character – to a point where there is no judgemental narrator at all. Her stream of consciousness technique challenges the very idea of authorial omniscience and a clear moral viewpoint. In his seminal work of literary criticism, *Mimesis: The Representation of Reality in Western Literature,* Eric Auerbach says:

The writer as narrator of objective facts has almost completely vanished; almost a common desire to represent the inner workings of the mind.

In Woolf's case, the individual's "stream of consciousness" is a mixture of retrospect and anticipation, with anticipation, as David Daiches puts it, "depending on and produced by retrospect, with the present moment simply the flow of one into the other". Just as in *Ulysses*, Joyce takes a chronological framework of less than 24 hours, but by probing into the mental states of his characters manages during that time to present to the reader most of their past history, so Virginia Woolf in *Mrs Dalloway* escapes from the limitations of chronology by the effective use of the "monologue intérieure". In his useful analysis of Woolf's style, Daiches argues that she is more courteous to the

everything stated appears by way of reflection in the consciousness of the dramatis personae... there actually seems to be no viewpoint at all outside the novel from which the people and events within are observed, any more than there seems to be an objective reality apart from what it is in the consciousness of the characters.

The American critic Reuben Brower argues that Woolf "moves from one narrative plane to another via image and metaphor", using the poetical and rhythmical abilities of language itself as a means of moving her story along. In the 1960s, Leon Edel similarly argued that Woolf's stream of consciousness technique was distinguished by her "brilliantly evocative prose-poetry" ∎

reader than Joyce; she had a tidy mind and signposts much more clearly than he does what she is doing.

When we are within a character's consciousness, Woolf constantly reminds us of the fact, with helpful repetition of phrases like "so it seemed to her" and "she thought, walking on". She also often uses the little word "for" to introduce a new turn in a reverie – and to indicate not a strict logical sequence but rather the half-logic or what Daiches calls the "pseudo-logic" of reverie, "the deep unconscious logic connecting... apparently random thoughts that crowd the drifting mind". When Clarissa is thinking about Peter Walsh, for example, she reflects:

> *... that was only her dear Peter at his worst; and he could be intolerable; he could be impossible; but adorable to walk with on a morning like this...*
> *For they might be parted for hundreds of years, she and Peter; she never wrote a letter and his were dry sticks, but suddenly it would come over her, if he were with me now what would he say?*

When we move from one character to another, the moment is always clear, often emphasised by the striking of a clock – usually Big Ben. So, in *Mrs Dalloway*, "we are either moving freely in time within the consciousness of an individual, or moving from person to person in a single moment". The sense of past and present being indistinguishably mingled is helped, says Makiko Minow-Pinkney in *Virginia Woolf and the Problem of the Subject*, by her deliberately inconsistent use of tenses. When Peter Walsh recalls a painful encounter with Clarissa at Bourton, he protests: "No, no, no! He was not in love with her any more!" – not "He had not been in love..." And again: "She came into the room; she stood..." – not "She had come into the room; she had stood..." The discourse then returns to the present with the narrator using the same past tense as has been

BIG BEN

According to Paula Goddard, writing in *History Today*, Big Ben (which first struck in 1859) "was first heard over the radio on New Year's Eve, 1923, when its chimes were broadcast at midnight to announce the New Year". From February 17th 1924, it could be heard every hour on BBC radio, along with "a regular time signal service from the Greenwich Observatory [which] was broadcast as a series of electronically produced 'pips'" every hour the BBC was on air. The cumulative effect was to make Londoners more aware of the passing of time.

When Peter Walsh follows a girl through Mayfair her "thin long cloak" stirs as she walks past "Dent's shop in Cockspur Street". Significantly, the founder of Dent's shop, E..J. Dent, was the man who built both Big Ben and the primary Standard Timekeeper of the United Kingdom at the Royal Observatory, Greenwich ∎

used to describe the remembered scene. The effect created is that the present and past are somehow fused together.

Woolf also gives her narrative cohesion by using linking devices such as the motorcar with drawn blinds which features in the first part of the book. This car, with its mysterious passenger, attracts the attention of those in the neighbourhood who see it:

> *The violent explosion which made Mrs Dalloway jump and Miss Pym go to the window... came from a motor car which had drawn to the side of the pavement...*
>
> *Edgar J. Watkins, with his roll of lead piping round his arm, said audibly, humorously of course:*

THE CINEMA

Virginia Woolf was fascinated by cinema, and, in 1926, wrote a thoughtful essay on the subject. It was the "imagistic" and "montage" features of the form (disconnected sequences of imagery designed to create an effect) which most interested her. "At first sight," she writes,

the art of the cinema seems simple, even stupid. There is the king shaking hands with a football team; there is Sir Thomas Lipton's yacht; there is Jack Horner winning the Grand National. The eye licks it all up instantaneously, and the

"The Proime Minister's kyar."
    Septimus Warren Smith, who found himself unable to pass, heard him.

The sky-writing aeroplane similarly attracts attention in different parts of London, enabling Woolf to move from one character to another, using the plane as a means of easy transition. That this linking device is cinematic is no accident: *Mrs Dalloway* was written in the early days of the cinema, a medium which strongly influenced Woolf. In the novel Peter Walsh ponders how young city workers will have "two hours at the pictures" before it gets dark, and during the party at the end the young socialites Lord Gayton and Nancy Blow also talk about the movies.

brain, agreeably titillated, settles down to watch things happening without bestirring itself to think.

Cinema's joyous release from "realism" – portraying life as it is, "literally" (what Aristotle called mimesis, or 'imitation') – offered her a sense of new narrative possibilities. It created a new connection between "eye and brain". The "flicks", as they were called, created what Woolf calls a "secret language" – the language of suggestive imagery.

If a shadow at a certain moment can suggest so much more than the actual gestures and words of men and women in a state of fear, it seems plain that the cinema has within its grasp innumerable symbols for emotions that have so far failed to find expression.

It was a project very close to her own ■

Mrs Dalloway may be a novel where our grasp of characters' lives is sketchy, but the material world is very much in evidence, as the cinematic images remind us. Woolf's interest in the nature of consciousness in *Mrs Dalloway* is balanced by a deliberate emphasis on the bourgeois solidity of the London world in which it is set. To read *Mrs Dalloway*, says Valentine Cunningham, is to be plunged into "the dense turmoil of central London shops, streets, parks, and things, things, things – frocks, gloves, hats, mackintoshes, umbrellas, breadknives, bodies, planes, cars, vans". What's wonderful about Woolf's writing, says Cunningham,

> is its celebration of people's selfhood in vivid relation to what's around them, especially the very ordinary stuff of existence. The more trivial the things people relate to, the more sharply do those things come to signify a potent access to the necessary heart of life – Mrs Dalloway's green dress, it might be, or her yellow hat, or the hats Rezia Warren Smith makes, the Bartlett Pears Walsh confidently orders at dinner, the things in Bond Street shops (and *Mrs Dalloway* started life as the story "Mrs Dalloway in Bond Street"), or that pell-mell of kitchen stuff in the Dalloways' basement at Party time.

Yet Woolf's real interest is in the way these things

are seen, and misunderstood or misinterpreted. The "materialist confidence" of her presentation of things is undermined by her emphasis on the unreliability and quirkiness of her characters' impressions. "The deluded visions of Kilman and Smith and of Peter Walsh snoozing in the park, are exemplarily unreliable." Septimus hears birds speaking Greek (as Woolf herself is said to have done); leaves and grass are alive for him, as sky and trees have womanhood for Peter Walsh – the kind of delusions the Romantic critic John Ruskin had in mind when he talked of the "pathetic fallacy". Misreading in the novel is everywhere. The sky-writing scene, says Cunningham,

> has become one of the great exemplary representations of modernist doubt about reading. Language is dying as we and the novel's Londoners look vainly on. Blaxo? Kreemo? Toffee? "What word was [the plane] writing?" Nobody will ever know.

Mrs Dalloway makes much of the contrast between the supposed solidity of things and the characters' tenuous grasp of them. It is a contrast that lies at the heart of the book. What Cunningham calls the book's "wonderful radical thinginess, as democratic as Dickens's" – set against the sense the novel gives of how unreliable and unstable people's perceptions can be – gives

Mrs Dalloway its ballast. It is one of the great successes of Woolf's novel.

What view of personality emerges from *Mrs Dalloway*?

The splintered narrative voice in *Mrs Dalloway* parallels and reflects the state of being which Virginia Woolf is trying to describe. Retiring to her bedroom after her morning errand to New Bond Street, Clarissa gazes into the mirror:

> *She pursed her lips when she looked in the glass. It was to give her face point. That was her self – pointed; dartlike; definite. That was her self when some effort, some call on her to be her self, drew the parts together, she alone knew how different, how incompatible and composed so for the world only into one centre, one diamond, one woman who sat in her drawing-room and made a meeting-point, a radiancy.*

Mrs Dalloway is "as thorough a meditation on the nature of self and identity as there is in fiction", says the American critic Perry Meisel. In the passage above, creating a sense of selfhood is described as an achievement – something to be accomplished. The way Woolf divides "herself" into two words suggests that the creation of a "definite" self "composed... into one centre" is the result not of a natural process of development but of discipline and effort. To create a coherent personality, Clarissa has to draw "the parts together" – and she does this by looking at her image in the looking glass. "With the mirror," says Meisel, "she gains in her reflection what she does not possess organically, a whole version of herself..."

But this mirror image is only that – an image. Clarissa's identity is composed of different elements which she has had to learn to blend together. The two primary ones, of course, are "Clarissa" and "Mrs Dalloway", with each proper name, says Meisel,

> signifying a different cluster of the various and incompatible "parts" that constitute her "own" or "proper" self – under the rubric "Clarissa", for example, her memories of Bourton, her relationship with Peter Walsh, her sexual fascination with other women, and so on; under "Mrs Dalloway", her marriage to Richard, her daughter Elizabeth, her role of hostess, and so on.

As Mrs Dalloway, she has to behave and feel in all sorts of ways, which are not required when she can return to thinking of herself as Clarissa. But she senses that she lacks a centre – "something central which permeated," as she puts it. This absence is not peculiar to her, though she thinks it is: rather, says Meisel, it is built into Woolf's conception of character as an image quite separate from the self it defines.

Clarissa's reverie, and her retirement to her attic room where she looks in the mirror, is

MRS DALLOWAY'S LONDON STROLL

The first, and most vibrant, section of *Mrs Dalloway* chronicles the heroine's expedition to get flowers for her evening party. One of the incidental pleasures for those who love this novel is to retrace her steps – either on a map, or, ideally, by foot on some bright June morning.

Woolf originally called her novel "The Hours" and

Clarissa's walk is precisely measured by the chimes of two prominent London clocks: Big Ben and that of the parish church of the House of Commons, St Margaret's. (When parliament sits Clarissa and her husband, Richard, live in the precincts of Westminster.)

Her first task is to cross busy Victoria Street. It is already hot. Big Ben is chiming ten o'clock behind her, and she is carrying a parasol (which adds an edge to the "fear no more the heat o' the sun" refrain in the narrative).

Having crossed the road, she "enters the park" – St James's Park, we deduce, just to the south of the Mall and prompted by the discovery that she has been excluded from Millicent Bruton's lunch party. The exclusion heightens her sense of insubstantiality, of social invisibility; she is left

feeling herself suddenly shrivelled, aged, breastless, the grinding, blowing, flowering of the day, out of doors, out of the window, out of her body and brain which now failed.

Green Park. Having crossed the park, along shady Queen's Walk, she faces another obstruction to cross – Piccadilly and its thundering omnibuses. She is standing at the Green Park gates, with the Ritz to her right, and Green Park tube station on her left. It will, have taken her, so far, some 25 minutes.

She next turns right down Piccadilly, remaining on the south side to browse in the window of Hatchard's bookshop – still there, physically unchanged since Clarissa gazed at its display of new, 1923 books (Lytton Strachey's *Queen Victoria*, which Woolf helped with, would have had pride of place). She does not go into the shop. She crosses the road into Bond Street (the most fashionable shopping street in the West End).

Bond Street "fascinates" her – a place of pearls, the very best gentleman's outfitters, and delicacies. She stops to look at the salmon in a fishmongers and a ladies' glove shop before arriving at her destination, Mulberry the florists, at the junction of what is now New Bond Street with Brook Street. Her purchase of the flowers (from the obnoxious, red-handed assistant, Miss Pym) is interrupted by what she at first thinks is a pistol shot, but is a car backfiring.

It is not described, but we may assume she returns to Victoria Street, and home, by taxi. Her "lark" is over ▪

Woolf uses the image of a house – a man-made structure – to describe the ebbing of Clarissa's sense of self. Later, the movement of Peter Walsh's mind is also described in terms of a house, "as if inside his brain by another hand strings were pulled, shutters moved". If strong selfhood is a secure house then the manner of Septimus's death – throwing himself from a window – is a sign of what he has failed to achieve.

Woolf was criticised by contemporaries for failing to create "character", but her failure, if so, is deliberate. She was challenging what, to her, was the conventional male view of "reality" and "character" and seeking to undercut what she called "the masculine point of view which governs our lives, which sets the standard.... which soon, one may hope, will be laughed into the dustbin where the phantoms go". Woolf was sensitive to the criticism, however. "I dare say it's true... that I don't have that 'reality' gift. I insubstantiate, willfully to some extent, distrusting reality – its cheapness. But to get further. Have I the power of

* What Woolf calls "the masculine point of view" is nowadays often referred to as the "male gaze", following a seminal 1975 essay by Laura Mulvey on the ways in which cinema, in particular, gives a privilege to the eye of the man, "objectifying" the woman. Woolf's belief that the "true reality" was reality for women has also become a prime tenet of modern critical feminism following Elaine Showalter's immensely influential study, *A Literature of their Own* (1977) – the title consciously echoing Woolf's *A Room of One's Own*.

conveying true reality?" The "true reality", to Woolf, was reality for women.[*]

In writing the novel Woolf aspired, she said, to be "only a sensibility"; her interest was in "the scattered parts" of people's characters and the process by which they assemble them into a plausible persona. It is no wonder, perhaps, that the critic Phyllis Rose calls *Mrs Dalloway* "the most schizophrenic of English novels". Whether walking through London or alone in her attic, Clarissa is mostly presented in a state of being where she does not need to "draw the parts together". Given her feeling of being scattered, or unassembled, it is interesting to note how obsessive she is about shoes and gloves: "old Uncle William used to say that a lady is known by her shoes and her gloves... Gloves and shoes; she had a passion for gloves." It is as if, says the critic Makiko

WOOLF ON PROUST

"[Marcel] Proust so titillates my own desire for expression that I can hardly set out the sentence. Oh if I could write like that! I cry. And at the moment such is the astonishing vibration and saturation and intensification that he procures – there's something sexual in it – that I feel I can write like that, and seize my pen and then I can't write like that. Scarcely anyone so stimulates the nerves of language in me: it becomes an obsession" ∎

Minow-Pinkney, "without this minute, 'passionate' attention the extremities of the body cannot be trusted not to fly asunder, acting out the physical dissociation their owner so often experiences..."

Clarissa, we are told, won't say of anyone "they were this or were that". Identity is never clear; she herself is never *just* one thing or the other.

> *She felt very young; at the same time unspeakably aged. She sliced like a knife through anything; at the same time was outside, looking on.*

Walking through London, her dispersed parts seem to fuse, for a moment, with objects she passes as she walks, and she becomes rhythm, sound, colour, shape. Even the sense of the body as a whole disappears: "this body she wore... with all i ts capacities, seemed nothing – nothing at all. She had the oddest sense of being herself invisible; unseen; unknown."

After she has studied her image in the mirror, pulling the scattered "parts" of her character together, she sits down to mend a silk dress and the focused "centre" or "diamond" of her consciousness dissolves again. She becomes as one with the physical rhythm of what she is doing.

> *So on a summer's day waves collect, overbalance, and fall; collect and fall; and the whole world seems to be saying "that is all" more and more ponderously,*

until even the heart in the body which lies on the beach says too, that is all... the body alone listens to the passing bee; the wave breaking; the dog barking, far away barking and barking.

What is true of Clarissa is true of other characters, too, especially Septimus. He experiences his body as "connected by millions of fibres" with the leaves of trees, and the sea imagery evoked during Clarissa's dress-mending recurs when he lies on the sofa in his sitting room: "the sound of water was in the room, and through the waves came the voices of birds singing". Unlike Clarissa, however, Septimus hasn't retained the power to fashion a coherent whole out of the scattered parts of consciousness. This is what separates them. "One cannot go on living with the self in abeyance, for this is the dividing line between sanity and madness," says Minow-Pinkney.

Clarissa, while able to assemble herself into a coherent person, sees the ego which she creates as essentially possessive and domineering – and her decision not to marry Peter Walsh is her rejection of masculine egotism. The secret space within Clarissa's self is symbolised by the attic to which she ascends "like a nun withdrawing, or a child exploring a tower". The two images convey the ambivalence of the attic, at once a place of deathly renunciation and excited new life and discovery. The scene is central to the novel: she mounts the stairs, we are told in an image which foreshadows the last chapter, "as if she had left a party... had shut the door and gone out and stood alone, a single figure against the appalling night". She takes off her feathered yellow hat as if discarding her social pretensions.

Clarissa's withdrawal to her attic room is ostensibly caused by her bad heart, but this illness has been exploited by both her and her husband for their own ends. "Richard insisted, after her illness, that she must sleep undisturbed." But Clarissa trumps this: "really she preferred to read of the retreat from Moscow. He knew this." The final curt sentence carries a stinging rebuke for her husband. In the same way, we are told that when Richard goes to bed he "as often as not, dropped his hot-water bottle and swore! How she laughed!" The point here may simply be that he is always rather drunk at night, though Minow-Pinkney thinks there is malice in the laughter, "as if Clarissa were mocking the feeble substitute (hot-water bottle) for the female bodily warmth she is denying him". She feels she has failed her husband, that her spirit has, in some way, contracted and grown cold, and this is reflected in the book she is reading about the Napoleonic retreat through snow.

But she rejects Peter Walsh, too, the man she might have loved. She is busy mending her dress when he arrives. She hears him at her door and "made to hide her dress, like a virgin protecting chastity". A subdued note of sexual violation pervades the scene. "'And what's this?' he said, tilting his pen-knife towards her green dress." To Minow-Pinkney, this fondling of the penknife suggests his insecurity, while Clarissa's sewing up of the dress "becomes the restitching into wholeness of a hymen which Walsh constantly threatens to tear".

Why does Clarissa suffer from a sense of loss?

During her reverie in the attic – and throughout the day – Clarissa is haunted by the dirge from *Cymbeline*:

> Fear no more the heat o' the sun
>> Nor the furious winter's rages;

The heat of the sun stands for sexuality – or, in Elaine Showalter's phrase, for "a kind of feminine blossoming and ripening which peaks in the heat waves of the June day and of the reproductive cycle, and ends in the furious winter of old age". The female lifecycle is a central preoccupation of *Mrs Dalloway*, and the female characters are at different stages of it. Millicent Bruton is 62, but dreams of being a little girl in Devon; Clarissa and

Sally Seton are in their fifties; Doris Kilman is past 40; Lucrezia Smith is in her twenties; Elizabeth, Clarissa's daughter, is almost 18. She is a "hyacinth which has had no sun" – that is, a virginal flower, like a lily, as Sally Seton remarks.

The parallels between the sexual and natural cycles are reinforced by the colour of women's attire, almost always green. Elizabeth is "like a hyacinth, sheathed in glossy green"; despite being expensively dressed, the debutante Nancy Blow looks, at the party, as if "her body had merely put forth, of its own accord, a green frill"; Septimus is entranced by the memory of Miss Isabel Pole in a green dress walking in a square; Clarissa admires

THE MENOPAUSE

Virginia Woolf grew up in a world which took a dismal view of "change of life". Nowadays doctors are more enlightened, but then they tended to see it as a condition to be dreaded and feared as much as insanity and one which might even be allied to it. From the mid 19th century onwards, doctors had been warning that the menopause could cause depression, madness and even suicide.

In *The Psychology of Women*, published in 1924, Helene Deutsch offered a particularly grim description of the menopause, describing it as a hopeless process of decline. "Everything she acquired in puberty is now lost piece by piece; with the lapse of the reproductive service, her beauty vanishes, and usually the warm, vital flow of feminine emotional life as well" ▪

"lovely old sea-green brooches" at the jewellers, and her favourite dress is a "silver-green mermaid's dress". Even Doris Kilman wears a green mackintosh.

Clarissa's sexual reverie in the attic is prompted, partly at any rate, by her time of life. In a short story written before she novel – "Mrs Dalloway in Bond Street" – she is shown as a woman going through the menopause. This is referred to in the story, though not explicitly, when Clarissa compares herself with the ailing Milly Whitbread, who comes to London to see doctors about a vague woman's ailment:

> *Of course, she thought, walking on, Milly is about my age – fifty, fifty-two. So it is probably that. Hugh's manner had said so, said it perfectly – dear old Hugh, thought Mrs Dalloway, remembering with amusement, with gratitude, with emotion; how shy, like a brother – one would rather die than speak to one's brother – Hugh had always been, when he was at Oxford; and came over; and perhaps one of them (drat the thing!) couldn't ride. How then could women sit in Parliament? How could they do things with men?**

*The passage is particularly ironic, says Showalter, "in the contrast between Clarissa's adolescent internalisation of menstruation as a crippling obstacle to women's participation in public life, and the change which took place after the war, when for the first time, there were indeed eight women sitting in Parliament".

This passage was revised in the novel, with the references to menstruation and menopause edited down to the level of the merest hint. But Clarissa's time of life ("T of L", as Woolf calls it in her diary) has, as Showalter puts it, "much to do with her sense of ageing, mortality and loss". The illness which has turned her hair white and left her a kind of nun "is a metaphor for the loss of fertility", for the unnameable "women's ailments" of her generation. Menopause, sometimes called the "little death" of women, couldn't be discussed in polite society in Woolf's day and was often implicitly linked with illness. Woolf herself, though only in her early forties when she wrote *Mrs Dalloway*, was obsessed with it – not surprisingly, perhaps, since she had been told by her doctors that she couldn't have children.

The preoccupation with childbirth and the end of child-bearing years shows in various ways: Sir William Bradshaw is introduced to us as a man who not only made England "prosper" and secluded her lunatics but "forbade childbirth"; Septimus feels a mad horror at the body and reproduction; Rezia longs for a baby; Clarissa, meanwhile, comes to terms with what Showalter calls "the finality of a central aspect of her identity". Clarissa has internalised the gloomy views about women's "change of life" prevalent in Woolf's day. She feels that her body, now that there is "no more marrying, no more having children", has become invisible, almost ceased to exist. The exclusion from Millicent Bruton's lunch party accentuates this, as we have seen, leaving her feeling "shriveled, aged, breastless", and triggering her lyrical meditation:

> *There was an emptiness about the heart of life; an attic room. Women must put off their rich apparel. At midday they must disrobe... Narrower and narrower would her bed be.*

THE WOOLFS AND CHILDREN

It's well-recorded that at the time of her marriage to Leonard Woolf, in August 1912, Virginia genuinely wanted children ("brats", as she fondly called them). Leonard, however, feared the "excitement" of pregnancy would trigger catastrophic mental breakdown. By the early 1920s, at the period she was writing *Mrs Dalloway*, both partners confided to different friends, that their marriage was "chaste" – celibate. Neither party was woundingly unfaithful to the other. (Leonard was complaisant about his wife's affair with Vita Sackville-West.) It was merely that sex had been turned off.

Leonard seems to have been the dominant partner in this suspension of full marital intimacy, supported by medical advice. After her menopause, Virginia told a friend she regretted not having forced Leonard to take the risk, "in spite of doctors". The unborn children made her "wretched in the early hours" ∎

The passage echoes the Fool's last speech in *King Lear*, "And I'll go to bed at noon." Clarissa, in her attic room, with a half-burnt candle, pauses "at midday" to consider the midpoint of her life, says Showalter.

> For women, Woolf suggests, the prime years are solitary, and empty as the womb; the female body sheds its "rich apparel" as the ageing woman must divest herself psychologically of her sexuality in preparation for death. The narrow bed, with its tight white sheets, where she "sleeps undisturbed", is a figure for the grave. This decline is Clarissa's equivalent of the wintry retreat from Moscow she reads about alone at night.

The most vivid memory of Clarissa's past is the girlish passion she felt for Sally Seton. Musing in her attic, she recalls her girlhood infatuation. For Sally, she felt "what men felt". There was excitement, ecstasy, and a kiss. This remembered love, says Showalter, seems to her "freer and richer" than anything she has ever felt for men. And now, seeking to understand the sexual dimension to her life that she feels has been irretrievably lost, she is conscious that she can no longer expect erotic pleasure to come to her. In Richard she has a loving and tender partner, but he has always been repressed, as repressed as she is, and they no longer even share a bedroom.

The way Clarissa broods about her lack of sexual responsiveness reflects, in part, a change in attitudes after World War One. The historian Susan Kent argues that on the one hand marriage seemed more important:

> British society sought in the establishment of harmonious marital relationships a resolution to the anxieties and political turmoil caused by the First World War.

On the other hand, women's expectations of marriage were growing, so

> discourses about female sexuality which before the war had emphasized women's lack of sexual impulse, and even distaste for sexual intercourse, underwent modifications to accommodate the political, social, and economic requirements of the post-war period. The new accent on motherhood was accompanied by a growing emphasis on the importance of sexual activity, sexual pleasure, sexual compatibility, between husband and wife.

As a number of critics have suggested, thinking of Clarissa as a menopausal woman makes the connections between her crisis and Septimus's seem clearer and more understandable. Woolf's original idea, when planning the novel, was to end it with Clarissa's death: "Mrs Dalloway was originally to kill herself, or perhaps merely to die at the end of the party." It's a reminder of the extent to which Woolf conceived of her heroine as a deeply depressed woman, sensitive to suffering despite the surface gaiety she shows the world. But while Septimus and Clarissa are linked through their mutual anxieties about sex and marriage, in the published novel it is Septimus who dies while Clarissa, less bleakly, reconciles herself to her lot. The novel implies, says Showalter, that menopause can involve "reintegration" as well as loss and can lead to growth if a woman confronts her anxieties about femininity, sex and identity. During the course of her day, Clarissa works through some of these feelings and comes to feel more at peace with "having done with the triumphs of youth".

Why is Clarissa's relationship with Sally Seton so important?

When Clarissa kisses Sally Seton it is "the most exquisite moment of her whole life". Her love for Sally – who "forgot her sponge and ran along the passage naked" – is "a sort of abandonment". Looking back, she is struck by its "purity" and "integrity"; it is the kind of female love, the novel suggests, impossible with a man. Sally teaches Clarissa about sex, speaks of sex in front of men and shocks people by running along the passage naked. In Clarissa's early experience of her, she boldly asserts herself as a woman, "as if she could say anything, do anything".

The relationship with Sally Seton, we are led to believe, is central to Clarissa's life and reflects the way Virginia Woolf views the world. Though insisting that the creative mind should be unimpeded by personal grievances, Woolf believed strongly that the distinctive perspectives of male and female writers always show through in their fiction. Women's experiences, she wrote in *A Writer's Diary*, are different from men's. "From this spring not only marked differences of plot and incident, but infinite differences in selection, method and style." Woolf expanded on this in *A Room of One's Own*: the values of women, she said, are often quite unlike

the values which have been made by the other sex; naturally, this is so. Yet it is the masculine values that prevail... And these values are inevitably transferred from life to fiction. This is an important book, critics assume, because it deals with war. This is an insignificant book because it deals with the feelings of women in a drawing-room. A scene in a battlefield is more important than a scene in a shop. Elsewhere, she witheringly called the First World War a "preposterous masculine fiction". So Woolf, one might argue, takes James Joyce's revision of the Ulysses myth and revises it again, this time feminising it.*

The setting is shops and drawing rooms, not battlefields, and instead of an epic quest there is what Elizabeth Abel calls "the traditionally feminine project" of giving a party. Meanwhile, the "potentially epic" plot of a soldier returning from war is demoted into a tragic subplot. (Woolf uses mock-heroic diction to satirise Clarissa's social world, as when Lucy the maid, "taking Mrs Dalloway's parasol, handled it like a sacred weapon which a goddess, having acquitted herself honourably in the field of battle, sheds, and placed it in the umbrella stand".)

If there are echoes of Joyce's novel in Woolf's – the events in both take place in a single city in a single day – there are also echoes of Jane Austen. Woolf hugely admired Austen – there is a hint of this, and also of Woolf's different preoccupations, in the way Clarissa mistakes her future husband's name, calling him Wickham (after the rakish

*When Peter Walsh arrives to see Clarissa, she is sewing, recalling Penelope's shroud in *The Odyssey*, which she knits by day, and unknits by night, to keep unwanted suitors at bay – until Odysseus arrives, not with a feeble penknife, like Walsh, but with a killing bow.

Wickham in *Pride and Prejudice*). Austen's plots revolve around courtship and end in happy marriages. In *Mrs Dalloway*, says Elizabeth Abel, Woolf "condenses the expanded moment that constitutes an Austen novel and locates it in a remembered scene thirty years prior to the present of her narrative, decentering and unraveling Austen's plot".

In *Mrs Dalloway*, marriage doesn't mean closure. The "courtship plot" is both evoked through memories and "indefinitely suspended in the present" as Clarissa replays in her mind her decision to marry Richard not Peter Walsh.

WOOLF AND VITA SACKVILLE-WEST

Virginia Woolf wrote *Mrs Dalloway* in the run-up to her passionate affair with Vita Sackville-West, and as critics have noted the excitement she felt is reflected in the description of Clarissa's feelings for Sally Seton. They met in 1922 but their affair didn't begin until December 1925.

Hermione Lee writes:
They cast each other, and themselves, in dramatic roles. Virginia set the terms, but Vita played up... Virginia was the will o' the wisp, the frail virgin, the "ragamuffin" or "scallywag", the puritan, the sharp-eyed intellectual... Vita was the rich, supple, luxurious, high-coloured, glowing, dusky, fruity, fiery, winy, passionate, striding, adventuring traveller... Virginia was the one with the head, Vita was the one with the legs ∎

It is mainly through Peter's memories, however, that we learn what happened – and of the slow and tortured end of the relationship. Clarissa's own most vivid memories, by contrast, are not of Peter but of Bourton, her childhood home, and her love for Sally Seton; absent, almost entirely, from these memories is Richard, whose wooing of Clarissa is presented entirely through Peter's painful recollections.

There is, then, a significant "narrative gap" in the novel. Between the Bourton scenes and the present – the June day in London – we can form only the barest outline of events. There are no details of Clarissa's marriage, the birth of her child

WOOLF'S FEMALE FRIENDSHIPS

Clarissa's experience at Bourton mirrors a part of Woolf's own. As an adolescent and in her early twenties, she had a series of intimate female friendships, including one with a family friend called Madge Symonds. A "romantic figure", she was, says Hermione Lee, "beautiful, intense, unconventional, dashing, sympathetic". She was "like an excitable child", wrote Woolf. A diary entry in 1921 – "I see myself now standing in the night nursery at Hyde Park Gate, washing my hands & saying to myself 'At this moment she is actually under my roof'" – mirrors the description of Clarissa's feelings for Sally in the novel ∎

or her move to London. We are told Clarissa never returns to Bourton after leaving it – emphasising the disjunction in her experience. It is her lost Eden. (Significantly, Bourton now belongs to a male relation.) Her life is now devoid of intimate female bonds: she hardly ever sees Sally, now Lady Rosseter; she is excluded from lunch at Lady Bruton's and competes with Miss Kilman for her daughter's allegiance.

Woolf, says Elizabeth Abel, "structures Clarissa's development as a stark binary opposition between past and present". In the narrative gap between Bourton and the present, and between Clarissa's memories and Peter's, there is a "clandestine" or "buried" story – a subtext which reveals Woolf's view of the way women develop, grow up and adjust to a patriarchal society

Woolf's view of female development is strikingly similar to Sigmund Freud's – coincidentally, *Mrs Dalloway* appeared in the same year (1925) as Freud's "Some Psychical Consequences of the Anatomical Distinction Between the Sexes". For years, Freud believed that boys and girls experienced what he named the "Oedipus complex" in similar ways: boys desired to possess (sexually) their mothers; girls their fathers. But in his 1925 treatise he offered a different theory – that female experience was more complex and difficult than male experience. While the male child, to develop into a mature adult, has to repress his erotic attachment to the mother, he is likely to go on desiring women, so at least he doesn't need to change his sexual orientation. The female child, on the other hand, has to change course dramatically. She goes through a pre-Oedipal stage; in the earliest days of her life she is bonded not with her father but with her mother. So she has to change the nature of her desire – to shift from mother to father – before renouncing it.

Freud, then, came to believe that girls have to switch the object of their erotic interest from women to men. They even, he thought, begin by experiencing a "masculine", clitoral sexuality focused on the mother, before switching to a passive, vaginal sexuality focused on the father. The route to female identity is therefore a circuitous one, or, as Freud himself put it,

> a comparison with what happens with boys tells us that the development of a little girl into a normal woman is more difficult and more complicated, since it includes two extra tasks [the change of sexual object and organ], to which there is nothing corresponding in the development of a man.

The idea that female development is very different from the male experience is implicit in *Mrs Dalloway*. Where Woolf parted company with

Freud was over the implications of this change. Freud believed that heterosexuality, marriage and motherhood were requirements for women's health and should be promoted; Woolf did not. In fact she believed the opposite, says Abel, as her treatment of Clarissa's attraction to Sally makes clear.

Clarissa's childhood is more or less omitted from the novel; we learn as little about what happens before the scenes at Bourton as we do about what happens after them. But the emotional tenor of the Bourton scenes, as Abel puts it, "suggests their representation of deferred childhood desire". What we are told of Clarissa's actual childhood amounts to a "tableau of female loss" – a dead mother and sister, a distant father, a stern maiden aunt, whose habit of pressing flowers beneath Littre's dictionary suggests to Peter Walsh, in its image of nature crushed, the oppression of women. Clarissa's earliest narrated memories are of Sally arriving at Bourton, and infusing the "formal, repressive atmosphere" with a vibrant female energy. Sally's uninhibited warmth and sensuality inspire 18-year-old Clarissa's love; Sally, says Abel, replaces Clarissa's dead mother and sister, her name even echoing the sister's name, Sylvia.

She nurtures Clarissa's passions and intellect, inspiring a love equal to Othello's in intensity and equivalent in absoluteness to a daughter's earliest bond with her mother, a bond too early ruptured for Clarissa as for Woolf, a bond which Woolf herself perpetually sought to recreate through intimate attachments to mother surrogates, such as Violet Dickinson: "I wish you were a kangaroo, and had a pouch for small kangaroos to creep to."

The passionate attachment Clarissa feels for Sally is the kind of attachment which, to Freud and other psychoanalysts and feminists, recaptures some of the intensity of the fractured mother-daughter bond.

> *The whole world might have turned upside down! The others disappeared; there she was alone with Sally. And she felt that she had been given a present, wrapped up, and told just to keep it, not to look at it – a diamond, something infinitely precious, wrapped up, which, as th walked (up and down, up and down), she uncovered, or the radiance, burnt through, the revelation, the religiou feeling! – when old Joseph and Peter faced them.*

Sally's kiss almost makes the earth move for Clarissa – "The whole world might have turned upside down!" She never forgets the "infinitely precious" moment. A Bourton she can't "take her eyes off Sally"; she is ecstatic about sleeping under the same roof; she feels "in love" with Sally and it is made clear that in the years which follow she yields to other women as well. The language of rapturous arousal Woolf uses to

*Natascha McElhone as the young Clarissa and Lena Headey as Sally Seton in
Marleen Gorris's 1997 film* Mrs Dalloway

describe Clarissa's feelings at these times, when
she feels for women "what men felt" for women, is
practically orgasmic:

> *It was a sudden revelation, a tinge like a blush which
> one tried to check and then, as it spread, one yielded
> to its expansion, and rushed to the farthest verge and
> there quivered and felt the world come closer, swollen
> with some astonishing significance, some pressure of
> rapture, which split its thin skin and gushed and
> poured with an extraordinary alleviation over the
> cracks and sores. Then, for that moment, she had
> seen an illumination; a match burning in a crocus;
> an inner meaning almost expressed. But the close
> withdrew; the hard softened.*

No writer before Woolf – or after her – has "so artfully turned the female body into such a rich source of metaphors for self-generation, ecstasy, illumination, self-transformation", suggests Patricia Cramer in "Virginia Woolf and sexuality", and this passage is a vivid example of her sexual style: "her reach for symbolic equivalence for female genitalia – the match and crocus for clitoris and labia; her emphasis on the quality of emotion aroused; and her deliberately crafted associations between female sexual ecstasy and female spiritual peaks of insight". Woolf's reference to Clarissa's "diamond... infinitely precious, wrapped up" – a metaphor for clitoral pleasures – is equally innovative, says Cramer. (Freud's writings pathologised clitoral in favour of vaginal orgasms.)

Freud believed homosexuality to be a mental illness, subject to cure. English literature before Woolf, even novels written by near contemporaries like Henry James and D.H. Lawrence, tended to depict lesbians as, in Cramer's words, "sinister predators slated for extreme loneliness, madness or death". Woolf, who wrote *Mrs Dalloway* in the run-up to her affair with Vita Sackville-West, the greatest romance of her life, felt quite differently.

Significantly, in the novel, Clarissa's lesbian passion for Sally precedes her relationships with men: the two women "spoke of marriage always as a catastrophe". Clarissa, at this point, sees Peter as an irritating intruder; the scene of her kiss is interrupted by his arrival with "old Joseph" (the unwelcome rupture is signalled typographically by a dash). Her reaction is dramatic.

> *It was like running one's face against a granite wall in the darkness! It was shocking; it was horrible!*

Clarissa is harsh about Peter's motives – "she felt his hostility; his jealousy; his determination to break into their comradeship" – suggesting to Elizabeth Abel an Oedipal configuration: the jealous male trying to break the exclusive female bond, insisting on the transference of attachment to the man, demanding heterosexuality. But this break, for women, is "as decisive and unyielding as a granite wall"; Clarissa takes revenge by refusing to marry Peter and instead settling for the less demanding Richard Dalloway "in order to guard a portion of her psyche for the memory of Sally".

Peter's interruption of Clarissa's love scene is paralleled, 30 years later, when he visits her at home in London: his emotional reunion with her is interrupted by her daughter, Elizabeth, unexpectedly opening the door and coming in. "Here is my Elizabeth," says Clarissa, her use of the possessive pronoun highlighting the intimacy of the mother-daughter tie and, in Abel's view, "the primacy of female bonds".

If Clarissa, despite her wrenching experience

with Sally, submits to the shift "from pre-Oedipal to Oedipal orientation", the disruptive effect on her life is suggested by the gap in her narrative – the gap between Bourton and the present. It is reinforced, too, by brief images of her sister and mother. Her sister, Sylvia, seems only to have been brought into the book to be destroyed. Peter recalls her death in an offhand manner. A young woman "on the verge of life", she is killed by a falling tree in an accident mysteriously associated with her father: "(all Justin Parry's fault – all his carelessness)". The shocking randomness of the death is reinforced by the way it is enclosed in brackets. It is like a distorted reminder, or echo, of Clarissa's split experience. The lack of any detail echoes, too, the long narrative gap in Clarissa's story. Her marriage, three decades of it, is simply blanked out. The pain of Clarissa's loss is thus hinted at but placed almost entirely outside the narrative.

Mrs Dalloway's buried, or clandestine plot suggests a view of female development strikingly similar to Freud's: it subverts, says Abel, "the notion of organic, even growth culminating for women in marriage and motherhood". The narrative gap challenges the convention of a linear plot – a linear plot, Woolf's novel suggests, is a distorted, regimented way of reflecting the subjective experience of women.

How are Clarissa and Septimus linked in the novel?

Virginia Woolf worried that reviewers of *Mrs Dalloway* would say it was disjointed "because of the mad scenes not connecting with the Dalloway scenes". The plot, it is true, doesn't connect Clarissa and Septimus, apart from the arbitrary link of Sir William (who conveys the news of Septimus's death to Clarissa at her party). But the connection between them is nevertheless intimate and vital, and in it, says Woolf's astute biographer, Hermione Lee, consists "the novel's most remarkable achievement". The similarity in the way Clarissa and Septimus respond to life makes us feel "that madness is an intensification or distortion of the method of perception that Virginia Woolf feels to be normal".

Their responses to experience are usually given in physical terms, and often quite similar terms. Here are two pairs of examples:

It rasped her, though, to have stirring about in her this brutal monster! to hear twigs cracking and feel hooves planted down in the depths of that leaf-encumbered forest, the soul; never to be content quite, or quite secure, for at any moment the brute would be stirring, this hatred, which, especially since her illness, had power to make her feel scraped, hurt in her spine.

Septimus heard her say "Kay Arr" close to his ear, deeply, softly, like a mellow organ, but with a roughness in her voice like a grasshopper's, which rasped his spine deliciously and sent running up into his brain waves of sound which, concussing, broke.

This gradual drawing together of everything to one centre before his eyes, as if some horror had come almost to the surface and was about to burst into flames, terrified him. The world wavered and quivered and threatened to burst into flames.

Why, after all, did she do these things? Why seek pinnacles and stand drenched in fire? Might it consume her anyhow? Burn her to cinders! Better anything, better brandish one's torch and hurl it to earth than taper and dwindle away.

Both Clarissa and Septimus translate their emotions into physical metaphors which, says Hermione Lee, "are indistinguishable from the emotion itself". The climax to this way of seeing things comes with Clarissa's reaction to Septimus's death: "her body went through it".

The difference between the two is that Clarissa, though reacting physically to things, never quite loses her sense that the outside world is separate to herself. She hears Big Ben striking and her thoughts are translated into a physical response: she "feels" the sound as "leaden circles" dissolving in the air, or as a bar of gold flat on the sea, or as a finger falling into "the midst of ordinary things". But she understands what the sound means; she doesn't think Big Ben is speaking to her. Septimus, on the other hand, while experiencing moments of sanity – "The upkeep of that motor car alone must cost him quite a lot," he says acutely after meeting Sir William – is constantly struggling to distinguish between his personal response and what Lee calls "the indifferent, universal nature of external reality". In Regent's Park he keeps trying to remind himself that the "shocks of sound" which assault him come from "a motor horn down the street" or "an old man playing a penny whistle". The difference between external reality and self is blurred in his ill mind,

...leaves were alive; trees were alive. And the leaves being connected by millions of fibres with his own body, there on the seat, fanned it up and down; when the branch stretched he, too, made that statement. The sparrows fluttering, rising, and falling in jagged fountains were part of the pattern...

Septimus's perceptions, argues Lee, "are those of a normal sensibility taken to its illogical conclusion". He is Clarissa's "double", a surrogate for her committing suicide on her behalf. It is as if Clarissa's potentially most dangerous and unstable impulses have been projected on to someone else – someone who can die for her.[*]

When first imagining Septimus, Woolf saw him as a madman who believed himself to be Christ and planned to assassinate the Prime Minister and become a political martyr. In revision she changed him into a former soldier suffering badly from shell shock. We are told that he was brave, that he was "one of the first to volunteer", that he "won promotion" during the War and that he "served with the greatest distinction". The reference to his "crosses" suggest, indeed, that he was a military hero, which makes the treatment he receives at the hands of his doctors all the more callous and unforgivable. On discovering he has leapt from his sitting room window, Holmes denounces Septimus as a "coward", but no label could be less appropriate. In flinging himself "vigorously, violently down on to Mrs Dilmer's area railings", he ends his life with the same belligerence he presumably showed on the battlefield.

Clarissa and Septimus survive both World War One and the deadly flu epidemic which followed it.

*As Elizabeth Abel points out, Woolf subverts the traditional 19th-century plot of "violently thwarted development" by substituting a hero for a heroine. Such heroines as Catherine Linton, Maggie Tulliver, Emma Bovary, Tess Durbeyfield and Antoinette Rochester all suffered and died. "By making Septimus the hero of a sacrificial plot that enables the heroine's development, Woolf reverses narrative tradition."

Their minds are similarly disordered; the connections between them proliferate as the novel unfolds.

Sir William would like to keep Septimus "in bed in a beautiful house in the country"; Clarissa, in a sense, is hospitalised too. She spends her nights in a "narrow" bed where her husband has "insisted, after her illness, that she must sleep undisturbed". There are other parallels. Clarissa still has a "small pink face"; Septimus's face was once "a pink innocent oval"; the old man who sees Septimus jump to his death has his counterpart in the "old lady" who lives opposite Clarissa and whom she sees on two occasions. Alone in his sitting room,

SEPTIMUS'S HEROISM

Being decorated with "crosses" for his bravery in World War One suggests that he had won at least medals. One of these may have been foreign – the French Croix de Guerre, the Italian Croce di Guerra, or the Belgian Military Cross – but it seems likely that at least one was British, probably the Military Cross. The other possibility (though rarely given) is the Victoria Cross, the highest award for heroism in battle.

It's complicated by the fact that we do not know Septimus's rank. The VC was open to all ranks, but only 600 or so were awarded in World War One. The MC (and DSO) were only awarded to officers of the rank of captain and above. If he were not an officer, Septimus might have won the Distinguished Service Medal or the Military Medal ▪

Septimus remembers hearing "dogs barking and barking far away..." Clarissa, alone in hers, has earlier also listened to a dog "barking, far away barking and barking".

Both characters are bird-like. Septimus is "beak-nosed" and reminds Lucrezia of "a young hawk"; Clarissa's face is "beaked like a bird's". Scrope Purvis thinks she has "a touch of the bird about her, of the jay". The screen in Septimus's room has "blue swallows" on it; Clarissa's drawing room curtains depict "a flight of birds of Paradise". Septimus is described as "hopping... from foot to foot" before he jumps from the window and, following his suicide, we are told that Clarissa's curtain "blew out and it seemed as if there were a flight of wings into the room". What David Bradshaw calls this "symbolic moment of

SHELL SHOCK

At Clarissa's party, Sir William Bradshaw discusses a Bill to deal with "the deferred effects of shell shock", and Septimus is a symbolic shell shock "case". The list of physical and psychological symptoms of shell shock was long and varied. "The symptoms were wildly diverse," writes Wendy Holden in her book on the subject. They ranged "from total paralysis and blindness to loss of speech, vivid nightmares, hallucinations and memory loss. Some patients declined eventually into schizophrena, chronic depression and even suicide."

Attitudes to shell shock

admission" happens before Clarissa hears of the suicide; it is as if Septimus's soul has arrived at the party through the open window. (To reinforce the idea, the curtain blows open twice more.)

Clarissa's "birds of Paradise" curtains evoke "the abode of the blessed", the Elysian fields from where the sparrows call to Septimus in Regent's Park and sing to him "in Greek words, from trees in the meadow of life beyond a river where the dead walk, how there is no death". Clarissa relives Septimus's violent death, connecting it to her own experience;

> *Then (she had felt it only this morning) there was the terror; the overwhelming incapacity, one's parents giving it into one's hands, this life, to be lived to the end... there was in the depths of her heart an awful*

varied widely too. At the War Office Committee of Enquiry into it which met from 1920 to 1922, E. MacPather testified that cowardice was "action under the influence of fear, and the ordinary kind of shell-shock, to my mind, was chronic and persisting fear". By this time, however, and even during the war itself, a minority of experts took a more enlightened view, and urged more compassionate treatment.

The historian Eric Leed argues in his book on World War One that the extraordinary range of symptoms of shell shock was "a psychic effect not of war itself but of industrialised war in particular". The horrors of the trenches, in other words, enforcing passivity and immobility, led to anxieties which could not be dissipated in action ■

fear. Even now, quite often if Richard had not been there reading The Times, *so that she could crouch like a bird and gradually revive, send roaring up that immeasurable delight, rubbing stick to stick, one thing with another, she must have perished.*

The final image recalls one of Septimus's "designs, little men and women brandishing sticks for arms, with wings – were they? – on their backs"; Clarissa's "awful fear" illustrates the Septimus-like vulnerability of her own mind.

Clarissa and Septimus are also linked by the quotation from *Cymbeline* – "Fear no more the heat o' the sun" – which Clarissa reads in Hatchard's shop window and which half-comes to Septimus as he lies in his room.

His hand lay there on the back of the sofa... Fear no more, says the heart in the body; fear no more.

The quotation can be seen as appropriate to both their situations. The lament in *Cymbeline* is spoken for Imogen, an outcast from her society, and an innocent victim of cruelty and lies. Isolation from society is what both Clarissa and Septimus, in different ways, experience in the novel. "'Fear no more the heat o' the sun' casts an air of serenity over the encounter with death to which the whole book leads up," says Hermione Lee. Despite the social gulf between them, Clarissa and Septimus are a pair: "the societified lady and the obscure maniac," wrote Woolf's friend, fellow novelist and confidant, E.M. Forster, "are in a sense the same person. His foot slipped through the gay surface on which she still stands – that is all the difference between them."

In her isolation, Clarissa is happier reading in her narrow bed than sleeping with her husband, while Septimus, we apprehend, has no interest in sex with his wife. In the same way, Clarissa's relationship with Sally may have its echo in Septimus's with Evans, the comrade who dies in battle. "Given the novel's insistent parallels between Clarissa and Septimus," says David Bradshaw, "the reader should consider whether Clarissa's homoerotic feelings for Sally are mirrored in Septimus's feelings for Evans." His grief for Evans, the officer who had shown him "affection" and in whom Septimus "had seen beauty", may even have contributed to his mental breakdown. Unable to feel anything after Evans's death, it is possible, says Bradshaw, that he "recoiled into heterosexuality (before the War he had idealised Miss Isabel Pole) and marriage with Lucrezia as a reaction to his feelings of grief and guilt about his compatriot".

Woolf may encourage the reader to believe there was a homoerotic element in the relationship between Septimus and Evans by stressing the Greek tie between the two men. Early in the novel, as we've seen, Septimus imagines the sparrows in Regent's Park singing to him in Greek. Later, in the moments before Evans appears from the bushes, he communicates with Septimus from behind a tree. "The dead were in Thessaly [a region of ancient Greece], Evans sang, among the orchids", and when Lucrezia brings home roses, Septimus thinks they have "been picked by [Evans] in the fields of Greece". As Linda Dowling has written, in the days before homosexuality was legalised, the "'love that dare not speak its name' could be spoken of, to those who knew their ancient history, as *paiderastia*, Greek love".

If Septimus is a repressed homosexual, the irony of segregating him to prevent his having children is even more tragic. But the text is by no means clear. Whatever Septimus's feelings for Evans, the novel suggests that his most intense feelings were for Isabel Pole, the upper class girl who introduced him to literature at Morley College. He is tormented by guilt over his fantasies about her – a girl, says Elaine Showalter, he had only wished "to respect, venerate and idolise". At the heart of his neurosis is not so much repressed homosexuality as a general horror of sex. "Unable to reconcile his unconscious desires with his strong feelings of propriety and even class superiority," says Showalter, Septimus has come to see "all sexual desire as evil and sordid".

TEN FACTS ABOUT
MRS DALLOWAY

1.

Eleven of the novel's 17 hours are spent with Clarissa, 10 with Peter, three with Septimus and six with the 116 minor figures representing the "English national character". (Nathalia Wright, "A Study in Composition", 1944)

2.

The kiss between Clarissa and Sally Seton, remembered as "the most exquisite moment of [Clarissa's] whole life", is the only kiss in Woolf's fiction.

3.

Mrs Dalloway was published by the Woolfs' own Hogarth Press (named after the area in Richmond, where they lived, and run from their dining room). Only 2,000 copies of the first edition were printed.

4.

The first American review of *Mrs Dalloway,* in the *New York Times* on May 10th, 1925, was short, found the heroine amiably "snobbish", and made no reference to either madness or Septimus Smith, but compared Woolf, favourably, to Mrs Humphry Ward (a novelist whom Woolf despised).

5.
A film of *Mrs Dalloway*, starring Vanessa Redgrave and Michael Kitchen and directed by Marleen Gorris, was released in 1997.

6.
In October, 2009, a first edition of *Mrs Dalloway* – with one of the rare dust jackets designed by Virginia's artist sister, Vanessa Bell – was auctioned by Swann Galleries for $18,000.

7.
"The Hours" – Virginia Woolf's working title for *Mrs Dalloway* (which she discarded) – was used by Michael Cunningham in his homage novel, published in 1998. This won a Pulitzer Prize and was made into an Oscar-winning film in 2002. Nicole Kidman played Virginia Woolf, with a cosmetically enlarged nose – the novelist's prominent facial feature.

8.
The only writer Virginia Woolf admitted to envying was Katherine Mansfield, whose story, "The Garden Party", was published in 1922, as Woolf began work on *Mrs Dalloway*.

9.

A commemorative bust was erected in 2004, in Woolf's Bloomsbury. The novelist, who had a morbid dislike of photographs of herself, would probably have disapproved.

10.

Between 1905 and 1907 Woolf taught composition, history and literature at Morley College For Working Men and Women, where Septimus is described as being a student.

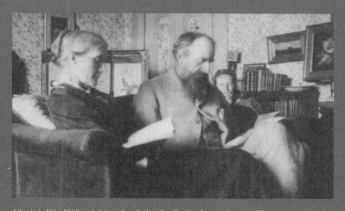

Virginia Woolf (far right) on her father Leslie Stephens (above): "There was something we had in common. 'What have you got hold of?' he would say, looking over my shoulder at the book I was reading; and how proud, priggishly, I was, if he gave his little amused surprised snort, when he found me reading some book that no child of my age could understand. I was a snob no doubt, and read partly to make him think me a very clever little brat. And I remember his pleasure, how he stopped writing and got up and was very gentle and pleased when I came into the study."

What does *Mrs Dalloway* tell us about British society?

Septimus is an acutely sick man. With his stammer, his loss of memory, delusions and generally disturbed behaviour, he shows many of the recognised symptoms of "shell-shock". Lucrezia realises her husband

> had grown stranger and stranger. He said people were talking behind the bedroom walls... He saw things too – he had seen an old woman's head in the middle of a fern.

He has suicidal tendencies, hears voices, jabbers back at them, sees a Skye terrier turning into a man, wants to tell the Cabinet that "trees are alive... there is no crime" and sees Evans coming towards him in Regent's Park.

But does shell shock account for all his symptoms? Or do his hallucinations, delusions of omnipotence and sense of guilt and martyrdom suggest something worse, namely schizophrenia? A voice tells him he is the messiah, "come to renew society"; the letters of the sky-writing plane are "smoke words... signalling their intention to provide him... with beauty, more beauty!" He feels light enough to fly, is convinced he can read people's evil thoughts and notes down revelations from the birds that sing to him. He believes he has been chosen to tell the secret truths of life to the Prime Minister and suffers terrible guilt, believing he has "committed an appalling crime and been condemned to death by human nature".

Woolf's finely detailed account suggests Septimus is not just a sensitive man traumatised by the war; he is suffering from a serious mental illness. The description of his sickness Woolf found hard to write, as it drew on her own memories of breakdown. "The mad part tries me so much, makes my mind squint so badly that I can hardly face spending the next weeks at it," she wrote in June 1923. Woolf's indignant representation of the kind of therapeutic advice Septimus receives from Doctors Holmes and Bradshaw reflects her own unhappy experience with doctors.

Woolf's harsh satire in dealing with the doctors, and the vivid description of Septimus's suffering, makes it easy to see him as the victim of medical power, and to think his suicide is a heroic act of defiance. But a close reading of the novel makes this view hard to sustain. Septimus has not only threatened to kill himself; he wants his wife to die with him. "Now we will kill ourselves," he tells her as they stand together by the river. David Bradshaw says that his flashes of sanity – as when he remarks on Sir William's expensive car –

suggest he is a "borderline case". Is he? Though Lucrezia is brave and loving, her husband is dangerous, and the doctors of *Mrs Dalloway* are probably right to recommend rest and seclusion.

This is not to deny that in their handling of Septimus they are insensitive and incompetent. The bluff, middle-class Holmes doesn't even get his diagnosis right, insisting that Septimus is merely "a little out of sorts" and believing that "health is largely a matter in our own control". He prescribes a dose of middle-class English masculine behaviour, including cricket, golf, music hall attendance and porridge.

The upper-class Bradshaw at least recognises the severity of Septimus's case, but while we are told his reputation is based on his "almost infallible accuracy in diagnosis... sympathy; tact;

NAMES

The doctors are well-named. Holmes, says David Bradshaw, has all the tenacity of Conan Doyle's sleuth – "Their only chance was to escape," thinks Septimus at one point, "without letting Homes know..." – but none of the perspicacity. He is completely clueless as to the nature of Septimus's illness. Sir William Bradshaw, who devotes a strict "three-quarters of an hour" to each of his patients, is named after the world-famous passenger train timetable, *Bradshaw's Railway Guide* (1831-1961). Like medicine, time is associated with authority and restraint in the novel.

Septimus Warren Smith

understanding of the human soul", there is little evidence of these last three qualities during his interview with Septimus. He interprets his patient's stuttering over the first person pronoun, for example, by seeing it as evidence of egotism. "'Try to think as little about yourself as possible,' said Sir William kindly. Really, he was not fit to be about."

Woolf said one of her aims in *Mrs Dalloway* was "to criticise the social system, and to show it at work, at its most intense". In the context of the novel, Septimus's illness, says Showalter,

> reflects the conditions of his society, one in which the after-effects of the war have been evaded, where Proportion [Bradshaw's watchword] is worshipped, and feelings have been numbed and anaesthetized.

has a curiously grand name for a poorly educated clerk. David Bradshaw wonders whether his "fantastic Christian name" was the one with which he was baptised – reflecting, with its Latinate ring, his parents' hopes of social advancement – or one chosen, with its two-part surname, by the aspirant poet himself. "Certainly there is no mention in the novel of any of the six older siblings the name Septimus implies, and the philoprogenitive connotations of his Christian name, coupled with the unavoidable association of 'Warren' with the teeming fertility of rabbits, serve only to spotlight the barrenness of his marriage." The lesbian, man-hating, Miss Kilman, is also aptly named; so is Scrope Purvis, the voyeuristic neighbour who watches her prepare to cross the street ■

The doctors' snobbish, tactless and callous behaviour is all part of this. The post-war world Woolf shows us is one in which the "governing classes" have been left oddly untouched; they continue their routines of civilised lunches, letters to *The Times*, well-meaning causes. None of the major upper-class characters has suffered a personal loss, or given a father, a husband, or son to the bloodshed (though we hear about Lady Bexborough, a minor character, "who opened a bazaar, they said, with the telegram in her hand, John, her favourite, killed"). Historically, of course, the truth was more or less the opposite. Young officers died in huge numbers in the trenches – it is estimated that one fifth of old boys from public schools were killed in the war.

But in *Mrs Dalloway* Woolf is intent on showing us the emotional repression she believed endemic in the upper echelons of English society. The novel is set very precisely on a day in June 1923, five years after the end of World War One. Peter Walsh, who has been out of England since the war, notes the transformation of society in that period:

Those five years – 1918 to 1923 – had been, he suspected, somehow very important. People looked different. Newspapers seemed different.

Politics was changing, too. By 1923, with the

eclipse of the Liberals, Labour was for the first time the official government opposition. Soon it would be in power. The Conservative Prime Minister who appears at Clarissa's party remained in office only until January 1924, when he was succeeded by the first Labour Prime Minister, Ramsay MacDonald. Richard Dalloway, a Conservative MP, anticipates this event; he plans to write a book about Lady Bruton's family when the Tories lose office.

The historical references, says the critic Alex Zwerdling, "suggest that the class under examination in the novel is living on borrowed time". Its values – what Peter Walsh calls "the public-spirited, British Empire, tariff-reform, governing-class spirit" – are under attack. Characters like Peter and Lady Bruton are identified with Britain's imperial mission, but the Empire is crumbling fast. In 1922 the last English troops left Dublin and the Irish Free State was born; there were stirrings in India, too. Peter Walsh goes to Clarissa's party not just to see her again but "to ask Richard what they were doing in India – the conservative duffers".

As a force, the class to which the Dalloways belong is in decline, says Zwerdling, and the party at the end of the novel is a kind of wake. "It reveals the form of power without its substance." When the Prime Minister finally arrives, he is described as looking "so ordinary. You might have stood him behind a counter and bought biscuits – poor chap, all rigged up in gold lace."

The imagery of this last section suggests rigidity and calcification. "Doors were being opened for ladies wrapped like mummies in shawls with bright flowers on them." Peter Walsh turns Miss Parry's glass eye into a symbol: "It seemed so fitting – one of nature's masterpieces – that old Miss Parry should turn to glass. She would die like some bird in a frost gripping its perch. She belonged to a different age." The picture we are given is one of a class impervious to change in a society that badly needs it. Lady Bradshaw is described vividly as "wedged on a calm ocean".

But it is the emotional obtuseness of Lady Bradshaw's class which has kept it in power, says Zwerdling. Threatening forces like Septimus and Doris Kilman are excluded and sequestered.

The political activities of the novel – Richard's committees, Lady Bruton's emigration project, Hugh Whitbread's letters to *The Times* and the ritual appearance of the Prime Minister – are essentially routine in nature. It is only by ignoring the deep scars of recent history that the "social system" keeps functioning: there may be a necessary connection in unstable times between traditional political power and the absence of empathy and moral imagination.

The governing class in *Mrs Dalloway* worships what Sir William Bradshaw calls "Proportion",

Nicole Kidman as Virginia Woolf in Stephen Daldry's 2002 film, The Hours

which is really the repression of instinct and emotion. In his book *Virginia Woolf*, A.D. Moody points to the impulse in the class "to turn away from the disturbing depths of feeling, and towards a conventional pleasantness or sentimentality or frivolousness". Richard Dalloway finds it impossible to tell his wife he loves her; he even seems to find it difficult to say "I":

> *The time comes when it can't be said; one's too shy to say it... Here he was walking across London to say to Clarissa in so many words that he loved her. Which one never does say, he thought. Partly one's lazy; partly one's shy.*

To Moody, Clarissa, too, is a representative of her class: "if her life is a kind of non-life, so too is the life of her society as a whole".

Amidst the seemingly unruffled self-control of the ruling class, the characters who can't learn to restrain their feelings, like Septimus, Miss Kilman and even Peter Walsh, are in trouble. They are the outsiders. "There is a conspiracy to keep any kind of vividness, any intense life, at a safe distance." Significantly, Bradshaw's car is grey, with grey rugs and silver grey rugs to match what is described as "its sober suavity".

The sense of living in a cocoon is reinforced by the novel's treatment of servants. Lady Bruton floats gently on "the grey tide of service which washed round [her] day in, day out…" Servants are assumed to be part of the natural way of things, as Woolf's description of the lunchtime ritual in Mayfair makes clear. "And so there began a soundless and exquisite passing to and fro through swing doors of aproned, white-capped maids…" Clarissa mentally thanks her servants "for helping her to be… gentle, generous-hearted"; but we see the cook struggling downstairs during her party:

Did it matter, did it matter in the least, one Prime Minister more or less? It made no difference at this hour of the night to Mrs Walker among the plates, saucepans, cullenders, frying-pans, chicken in aspic, ice-cream freezers, pared crusts of bread, lemons, soup tureens, and pudding basins which, however hard they washed up in the scullery, seemed to be all on top of her…

Woolf makes us see the connection between "the elegance and composure of the governing class and the ceaseless activity of the lower", says Zwerdling. But if there is a gulf between servants and their employers there is also a gulf between the people who belong to Clarissa's set and those who don't. Although she defends her parties as an expression of unity – bringing together "so-and-so in South Kensington; someone up in Bayswater; and somebody else, say, in Mayfair" – the Septimus Smiths and Doris Kilmans are shut out, as, mostly, are artists. Despite the presence of a token poet at the party, Clarissa's social world is a largely philistine one.

Richard says, stuffily, "no decent man ought to read Shakespeare's sonnets because it is like listening at keyholes (besides, the relationship was not one that he approved)".* Sally says of Hugh Whitbread that "he's read nothing, thought nothing, felt nothing"; Sir William "never had time for reading"; Lady Bruton, though Lovelace and Herrick once came to her country estate, "never read a word of poetry herself". In *Mrs Dalloway*, says Zwerdling,

> an obsession with Shakespeare (as in the thoughts of Septimus and Clarissa) is a kind of shorthand indication that the soul has survived, that some kind of sympathetic imagination is still functioning.

Is there something contradictory and self-indulgent in Woolf's attack on the governing classes? Many readers have thought so, including the Marxist intellectual Raymond Williams – the contradiction, to Williams, is characteristic of Bloomsbury as a whole. Woolf and her fellow intellectuals were lucky beneficiaries of the very

*He may be thinking of Oscar Wilde's detection, in his story, The Portrait of Mr W.H., of homoeroticism in Shakespeare's sonnets.

capitalist society which they condemned; their own position of privilege gave them the luxury to indulge their existential anguish; and hand in hand with their attacks on the bourgeoisie went a not very well disguised sense of superiority.

Miss Kilman denounces Clarissa ("She came from the most worthless of all classes – the rich, with a smattering of culture..."), but she herself is shown to be agressive and unpleasant. Makiko Minow-Piney thinks she represents the middle-class fear of the lower orders as a mob, "clamouring for gratification". Hence the novel's stress on her voracity: her wolfing down of éclairs, her desire for the sensory pleasures of which she has been deprived.

The novel treats Clarissa with much more sympathy than it does Miss Kilman. Indeed it is "greatly enamoured" with Clarissa's social world, says Valentine Cunningham, "and does rather endorse her disgust over poor Doris Kilman's shabby green mackintosh, and her wish that Elizabeth was more interested in gloves and less in religion". But to Cunningham, the novel's "snootiness", its commitment to Clarissa's "upper-class reckonings and her limited sense of the ordinary", is the "incidental downside" of the extraordinary and vivid picture of London life Woolf creates in the novel.

And Clarissa, after all, has good reason to loathe Miss Kilman. She despises the way the tutor tries to convert her daughter, Elizabeth, to her enthusiastic form of Christianity. (Clarissa herself, like her creator, is an atheist. "Not for a moment did she believe in God.")

> *The cruellest things in the world, [Clarissa] thought, seeing them clumsy, hot, domineering, hypocritical, eavesdropping, jealous, infinitely cruel and unscrupulous, dressed in a mackintosh coat, on the landing; love and religion. Had she ever tried to convert anyone herself? Did she not wish everybody merely to be themselves?*

Miss Kilman's dogma, her bitter Christian socialism, with its overtones of Victorian evangelism, and her 'conversionist' – coercive – efforts echo William Bradshaw's love of "proportion" and Lady Bruton's imperial eugenicism. She is seen as suffering from a blind, hypocritical adherence to ideals.

> *Miss Kilman would do anything for the Russians, starved herself for the Austrians, but in private inflicted positive torture.*

How does the novel connect doctors with British imperialism?

Mrs Dalloway is much concerned with the power of the state – how it operates, who exercises it and to what extent it can be escaped. In his study of Virginia Woolf, Michael Whitworth notes that the chimes of Big Ben spreading across London, and the "leaden circles" dissolving in the air, draw attention to the theme of the radiation of power. Authority enforces conformity, as in, for example, the passage which links "Proportion" to "the clocks of Harley Street".

Sir William Bradshaw, obsessed by "proportion", is the foremost symbol of authority. Woolf draws attention to the similarities between his power over his patients and the power of the Empire over its subjects. Backed up by the "police and the good of society", we are told, his patriotic toil is unending:

> *Worshipping proportion, Sir William not only prospered himself but made England prosper, secluded her lunatics, forbade childbirth, penalised despair, made it impossible for the unfit to propagate their views until they, too, shared his sense of proportion... But Proportion has a sister, less smiling, more formidable, a Goddess even now*

*engaged – in the heat and sands of India, the mud
and swamp of Africa... in dashing down shrines,
smashing idols, and setting up in their place her own
stern countenance. Conversion is her name and she
feasts upon the wills of the weakly, loving to impress,
to impose, adoring her own features stamped on the
face of the populace.*

"Conversion", as it is used here, means "political
indoctrination", and this passage – in which the
narrator is unusually intrusive and didactic –
explicitly links the handling of Septimus Smith
with British imperialism and social repression. At
the end of the novel, says Alex Zwerdling, it is
"entirely appropriate that this psychiatrist-
policeman and the Prime Minister should be
invited to the same party".

The analogy between the treatment of the
mentally ill and imperial power abroad is
underlined a few pages later, when we hear of Lady
Bruton's plans to export young British people to
Canada. Lady Bruton may be more ardent than Sir
William – she has "lost her sense of proportion" in
pursuit of her scheme – but she is full of the spirit
of "conversion", proportion's "less smiling" sister
which "feasts on the wills of the weakly". It is in
this spirit that she devises her own "feast" – turbot
in a rich sauce, chicken casserole, wine and coffee
– to garner support from Richard Dalloway and
Hugh Whitbread in her efforts to "impress" her

patriotic and eugenicist ideology on "the face of the populace" of Canada.

The lunch shows the Establishment at work. Lady Bruton's pet scheme is a project "for emigrating young people of both sexes born of respectable parents and setting them up with a fair prospect of doing well in Canada". But it needs Hugh Whitbread's skilful pen to make it sound palatable to an Establishment audience. He "possessed – no one could doubt it – the art of writing letters to *The Times*". His name "commanded respect". He "marvelously reduced Lady Bruton's tangles to sense". As Woolf knew, a letter to *The Times* advocating the emigration of

THE CANADIAN CRISIS

Canada faced all sorts of political and economic problems in the 1920s. Canadian eugenicists, according to the American academic Ian Robert Dowbiggin, tended to blame the mental deficiencies of immigrants, especially British immigrants. In a lecture in London in May 1923, the eminent Canadian eugenicist Charles Clarke, Professor of Psychiatry at the University of Toronto, "told his audience that immigration had pushed Canada to the brink of crisis. The country was being 'bled white' by immigration to the United States and pumped full of defective and 'mentally diseased' immigrants, many of whom were British".

In its account of his lecture, *The Times* reported that Clarke had made "a strong plea for the introduction to Canada of the respectable people to Canada would have gone down well in those days as a response to the unemployment and industrial strikes which shook England in the early 1920s, and which would culminate in the General Strike of 1926. In her attempt to "criticise the social system", Woolf is trying to show that what proportion and conversion really amount to is coercion.

Nigeria, South Africa and Ceylon are each mentioned briefly, but Canada and India are the countries taken to stand for the Empire in *Mrs Dalloway*. Lady Bruton, who "never spoke of England, but this isle of men, this dear, dear land" and who has "thought of the Empire always at

best Nordic types. He was not at all anxious to see his country flooded by hosts of people of inferior type. "It is all very well," he said, "for Rudyard Kipling and other enthusiasts to say that what Canada must do is pump in the population. That is true; but at the same time, it is necessary to put the suction-pipe in waters not polluted by defect, physical degeneracy and social failures". In an editorial, *The Times* endorsed Clarke's stance, taking a strongly hereditarian line: "weak or degenerate, and therefore potentially immoral types... are without question, the architects of slums and the perpetuators of the worst side of city life", whose children "tend to reproduce their evil traits. To exclude them from a population is, therefore, to secure that population against innumerable dangers and disasters."

Woolf was clearly aware of all this. Lady Bruton's letter, from the brief extracts we are given, reflects the views uttered by Clarke and approved by *The Times*. ∎

hand", worries about "the state of India" as well as her Canadian project. Peter Walsh, when he comes back after five years on the sub-continent, reflects: "All India lay before him; plains; mountains; epidemics of cholera; a district twice as big as Ireland." Yet, though his Anglo-Indian family have administered Indian affairs for three generations, he dislikes the country, and the Empire. His uncomfortable relationship with India is emphasised when we are told he orders "wheel-barrows from England, but the coolies wouldn't use them".

The Empire, Woolf suggests, is not just bad for the Indians, or those who administer it; it has a generally debilitating effect. The shoppers in Bond Street look "at each other and [think] of the dead; of the flag; of Empire", while a "Colonial"'s insulting remark about the Royal Family results in "words, broken beer glasses, and a general shindy" in a backstreet pub. Symbolically, when Miss Kilman gets lost in the Army and Navy Stores she becomes "hemmed in by trunks specially prepared for taking to India". The restriction of her life, says David Bradshaw, is shown to be connected "with the limitations which Britain has imposed on her Empire". Lady Bruton is handled satirically – she is a comic figure – but also with a shrewd feminist perception of what makes her tick. Strident, manly and "angular" she seems to embody the virtues of the imperial class. "She should have been a general of dragoons herself," thinks Richard Dalloway. She can't play a feminine role:

> *Lady Bruton raised the carnations, holding them rather stiffly, with much the same attitude with which the General held the scroll in the picture behind her...*

On the other hand, because she is a woman she can't be the general she wants to be either. Woolf accentuates the paradox by using phallic words to describe her posture ("ramrod"/"stiffly"), as if Millicent Bruton is struggling to get a grip of the masculine power which evades her:

> *her hand, lying on the sofa back, curled upon some imaginary baton such as her grandfathers might have held, holding which she seemed... to be commanding battalions marching to Canada...*

But the phallic references simply make her seem even more emasculated. Lady Bruton wants to be part of a patriarchal, military establishment that is structured against her. In espousing the very values of the establishment which constrains her life, then, she herself must share the blame for her own exclusion from it.

In this Establishment world, the three main characters in the novel, Clarissa, Septimus and Peter Walsh, are all, to different extents, outsiders

– all, as Michael Whitworth says, "resistant to the patterns imposed by authority". Septimus is the obvious outsider, while Clarissa, in her role as "Mrs Richard Dalloway", is part of political society but wields no actual power. Woolf's use of a mixture of free indirect discourse and "external reports", says Whitworth, convey both Clarissa's loneliness and her "complacent acquiescence" in the role she plays; the novel is "simultaneously sympathetic and satirical" about her. Her acquiescence is echoed in the short account of how Lady Bradshaw, after a short struggle, surrenders her will to that of her husband.

Fifteen years ago she had gone under. It was nothing you could put your finger on; there had been no

EMPSON'S COMPLAINT

The brilliant linguist and critic, William Empson, was scathing about Woolf's experimental use of language. The psychologising in *Mrs Dalloway* made him impatient: he wanted more plot – in particular, he wanted to be told about the meeting between Clarissa and Peter Walsh after the party. His analysis of a typical Woolfian paragraph mimics her style of inconsequential complication:

We arrive, for instance, with some phrase like "and indeed" into a new sentence and a new specious present. Long, irrelevant, delicious clauses recollect the ramifications of the situation (this part corresponds to the *scene, no snap; only the slow sinking, water-logged, of her will into his.*

Yet while in a way Clarissa, too, has "gone under" she remains able to examine her heart and her memories, and to challenge her understanding of herself. The novel distinguishes her from Lady Bradshaw and, pointedly and clearly, from Sir William: "...she did not know what it was – about Sir William, what exactly she disliked. Only Richard agreed with her, 'didn't like his taste, didn't like his smell'." Sir William, Clarissa understands intuitively, is "obscurely evil... capable of some indescribable outrage – forcing your soul, that was it".

Peter Walsh, back in England after years away

blurring of consciousness while the heroine waits a moment to know her own mind; and it is here, by the way, that one is told most of the story); then by a twist of thought some vivid but distant detail, which she is actually conscious of, and might have been expected to finish the sentence, turns her mind towards the surface. From then on the clauses become shorter; we move towards action by a series of leaps, each, perhaps, showing what she would have done about something quite different, and just at the end, without effort, washed up by the last wave of this disturbance, like an obvious bit of grammar put in to round off the sentence, with partly self-conscious, wholly charming humility in the heroine (how odd that the result of all this should be something so flat and domestic), we get the small useful thing she actually did do ■

from it, is both an insider and an outsider. Having been hundreds of miles from the centre of power, he returns to London to see it as an outsider. A dreamer and a fantasist, he is described as "not altogether manly". He follows a young woman from Trafalgar Square to Oxford Street, "stealthily fingering his pocket-knife", and reflects as he walks through Regent's Park: "This susceptibility to impressions had been his undoing, no doubt." The words "susceptibility" and "impressions" are key, says David Bradshaw: Peter's susceptibility is implicitly contrasted with a martial and masculine invulnerability; his sensitivity to impressions, in the gendered psychology of the time, was a feminine quality of mind. In *The Vocation of Women*, published in 1913, Mrs Colquhoun argued that the female mind "takes more impressions than the male, but leaps to hasty generalisations". For these reasons, the "impressionist" novel was taken by some of Woolf's contemporaries to be a feminine mode of writing.

"Behind his mask of masculine bravado," says Elaine Showalter, "is an immature man who cannot reconcile his alleged ideals with his real feelings and acts." While middle-aged women like Clarissa can live their lives vicariously through their daughters,

men have the chance to renew their lives through action; if women, as Walsh muses, seem to live more in the past, it is because their lives are more bounded and determined by choices made early in youth.

Walsh, however, is unable to take the chance to "renew" his life. More scarred by Clarissa's rejection of him than he likes to admit, he is deeply affected by the past. His constant fiddling with his pocket-knife, which Clarissa sees as silly and weak, suggests his frustration and timidity. The knife epitomises his "compromised rebellion", says Alex Zwerdling.

On the whole, the outsiders in *Mrs Dalloway* are distinctively thinner than the insiders. Clarissa has a "narrow pea-stick figure", Doris Kilman is gaunt, Septimus "was always thin" and his wife Lucrezia has grown "so thin" with worry. The Establishment figures, by contrast, are robust. Lady Bruton has a "robustness of demeanour". "Tall men, men of robust technique", peer out of the windows of White's and other clubs. It is wholly ironic, as David Bradshaw says, in view of Septimus's treatment, that Peter Walsh finds "wholly admirable" the way that "the doctors and men of business and capable women" all seem "punctual, alert, robust". In contrast, the young men who parade up Whitehall from the Cenotaph do "not look robust".

Like the "perfectly upholstered" Hugh Whitbread, the doctors are well padded: "Large, fresh-coloured, handsome", Holmes is a "powerfully built man". He and Sir William "never weighed less than eleven stone six" – hefty by the standards of the day. Sir William, we are told, believes that feeding up his patients is an important part of making them healthy.

Robust the Establishment figures in *Mrs Dalloway* may be, but they are not as grand as they think they are. Sir William believes that "unsocial impulses" such as those he discerns in Septimus are "bred more than anything by the lack of good blood". He has a "natural respect for good breeding..." Yet Sir William himself is the son of a shopkeeper. Richard Dalloway's daughter, Elizabeth, meanwhile, is described in such a way as to cast doubt on her – and, indirectly, her father's – breeding. Peter Walsh thinks her "a queer-looking girl" and her odd appearance is stressed more than once:

> *Was it that some Mongol had been wrecked on the coast of Norfolk... had mixed with the Dalloway ladies, perhaps a hundred years ago. For the Dalloways, in general, were fair-haired; blue-eyed; Elizabeth, on the contrary, was dark; had Chinese eyes and a pale face; an Oriental mystery...*

The attention paid to Elizabeth's appearance suggests that for all Richard Dalloway's admiration for pedigree and good blood, he seems unaware of his own family history. Woolf's point, says David Bradshaw, "is surely that, *pace* Bradshaw and Dalloway, pure breeding is pure tosh".

How can the individual escape authority in *Mrs Dalloway*?

Mrs Dalloway offers a convincing picture of centralised authority, but a less convincing one of how to escape or elude it. One image of escape is Clarissa's reverie about her adolescence at Bourton. It is not precisely dated, but Peter refers to "thirty years" having elapsed, so it may have occurred in the summer of 1893. Michael Whitworth sees this as significant: two years before Oscar Wilde's trial for "gross indecency" in 1895, "it implies the comparative sexual tolerance of that period, and not the more repressive atmosphere that prevailed after Wilde's 'fall'".

A similar period of freedom is imagined further back in the past. Rezia, feeling alone in Regent's Park, thinks back to a Britain in which, as in the darkness, "all boundaries are lost" – a Britain which "reverts to its ancient shape, as the Romans saw it, lying cloudy, when they landed, and the hills had no names and rivers wound they knew not where".* The novel, says Whitworth,

contains what we might call an "under-narrative",

an implied account of human history: once, when the Romans arrived, and again following the prosecution of Oscar Wilde, identities became fixed and choices became restricted; an imperialism of the spirit set in.

It is a nostalgic view, leaving the reader with the idea that there were periods of greater freedom in the past, and contributing to the elegiac tone of the novel. "The historical vista intermittently inserted in *Mrs Dalloway*," says Elizabeth Abel, "echoes the developmental progress of the heroine from a nurturing, pastoral, female world to an urban culture governed by men." This urban culture is seen as having become even more masculine since the war. Woolf's imagery and plot, says Abel,

> portray the world war as a vast historical counterpart to male intervention in female lives. In one pointed metaphor, the "fingers" of the European war are so "prying and insidious" that they smash a "plaster cast of Ceres", goddess of fertility and mother love, reminder of the force and fragility of the primary female bond. Rezia's female world is shattered by the conjunction of marriage and war.

*There is an echo of Conrad here – Marlow, the narrator of the anti-imperialist Heart of Darkness, imagines the Roman conquest of the Thames Valley, "...when the Romans first came here... darkness was here yesterday," he says. Woolf was an admirer of Conrad and wrote an essay on him in 1923.

The idea that World War One bolstered male authority lacks all historical validity – historically, it is as false as the idea that the carnage in France claimed few casualties among the aristocracy. Nevertheless, "within the mythology created by the novel", the war assumes a symbolic function, "dividing a pervasively masculine present from a mythically female past".

The only people who escape this post-war masculine authority are Septimus Smith, because he is insane, and the various beggars seen by Clarissa, Richard and Peter Walsh during the narrative. The beggars are unconvincing figures, treated more as "symbols of liberty" than real people, as Michael Whitworth puts it. This "tends to obscure their humanity and to erase the lives they led before becoming vagrants". Clarissa thinks the "dejected miseries" sitting on doorsteps "can't be dealt with... by Acts of Parliament"; Peter's account of the female beggar he sees in Regent's Park transforms her into a figure who has stood in the same spot for millions of years – an "extravagant reworking", says Whitworth, of the cliché that "the poor are always with us".

So – apart from becoming a beggar – what alternative to social conformity does *Mrs Dalloway* suggest? If one answer is a defiant individuality, it is hardly an adequate one. The character, after all, who takes defiance to its logical limits, escaping what Clarissa thinks of as the "corruption, lies, [and] chatter" of social life, is the one who commits suicide.

Whitworth writes: "To say that there was 'an embrace in death' is to say that we are all tragically alone in life; there is no possibility of a social system which is not oppressive." The choice between lonely individualism on the one hand and surrendering to an oppressive society on the other is an invidious one.

The novel, however, suggests another possibility: the idea that we can connect with others, even those we've never met, at a deeper level than society permits – that sensitive individuals are linked to each other and to the sentient world by a whole network of shared thoughts, sensations and feelings. The character who experiences this most is Clarissa. Like Peter and Sally Seton, she is part-conformist, part-rebel; she retains a private as well as a public self. She retains, too, the capacity to cherish solitude, a capacity Woolf thought profoundly important. A modern audience, she wrote in an essay on Elizabethan drama, has a need to explore the private as well as the public self. The "extravagant laughter, poetry, and splendor" of an Elizabethan play denies us something:

It is solitude. There is no privacy here. Always the door opens and someone comes in... Meanwhile, as if tired with company, the mind steals off to muse in solitude; to think, not to act; to comment, not to share; to explore its own darkness, not the bright lit-up surfaces of others.

It is privacy of this kind which Clarissa seeks when she withdraws from the party at the climax of *Mrs Dalloway*. The little room she retreats to is one where "the party's splendour fell to the floor, so strange it was to come in alone in her finery". It is here, says Alex Zwerdling, that Clarissa "allows herself to think about Septimus's death with full imaginative sympathy, understanding his feelings and situation instinctively with some part of her self that scarcely functions in the public world she normally inhabits". She realises that Septimus has managed to rescue in death an inner freedom that her own life is constantly forcing her to barter away:

> *A thing there was that mattered; a thing, wreathed about with chatter, defaced, obscured in her own life, let drop every day in corruption, lies, chatter. This he had preserved.*

In feeling what she does for Septimus, Clarissa, in her imagination, is moving beyond the narrow class-based world to which she belongs. In another of her essays, Woolf described what she called "The Russian Point of View". Dostoevsky, she said, is indifferent to class barriers.

It is all the same to him whether you are noble or

simple, a tramp or a great lady. Whoever you are, you are the vessel of this perplexed liquid, this cloudy, yeasty, precious stuff, the soul.

Though they have never exchanged a word, Septimus and Clarissa, on some deep level, are kin, the novel suggests. So, for all their mutual hatred, are Clarissa and Doris Kilman. On the point of withdrawing to her little room, Clarissa feels sudden contempt for her social triumphs. They "had a hollowness", she feels. In the same moment she recalls

Kilman her enemy. That was satisfying; that was real. Ah, how she hated her – hot, hypocritical, corrupt; with all that power; Elizabeth's seducer... She hated her; she loved her. It was enemies one wanted, not friends.

These reactions to Septimus and Kilman, says Zwerdling, together suggest Clarissa's soul "is far from dead, that she can resurrect the intense emotions of youth despite the pressure of a society determined to deny them quarter".

Clarissa's reactions are part of what has been called a theory of "group consciousness". Peter Walsh recalls Clarissa as a girl having a theory that her being was not confined to her physical location; her circle of sympathy was not restricted to people she'd actually met. The theory compensated for their shared feeling "of dissatisfaction; not knowing people; not being known". Clarissa had felt herself to be "everywhere", so that "to know her" one would have to seek out the people who "completed" her. "Odd affinities she had with people she had never spoken to: some woman in the street, some man behind a counter – even trees, or barns." Peter Walsh believes the theory explains why his own relationship with her has lasted, despite the fact that their actual meetings have been infrequent and often "painful". These meetings formed a

> *sharp, acute, uncomfortable grain... yet in absence, in the most unlikely places, [the relationship] would flower out, open, shed its scent, let you touch, taste, look about you, get the whole feel of it and understanding, after years of lying lost.*

As well as allowing Peter to interpret his own relationship with Clarissa, says Michael Whitworth, the "supersensory" theory allows the reader to understand what she means when she feels "somehow very like" Septimus, despite never having met him. The vocabulary and imagery of *Mrs Dalloway* reinforce this notion of "group consciousness". The Prime Minister's car creates "a slight ripple"; the leaden circles of Big Ben dissolve in the air; Clarissa becomes a plant on the riverbed. The avian characteristics shared by

Clarissa and Septimus are also evident in Sally Seton ("She seemed... like some bird"), Lucrezia ("[Septimus] watched her snip, shape, as one watches a bird hop..."), Peter Walsh, whose eyes are described as "hawk-like", and others. The dead are also associated with birds. As people look up at the sky-writing plane,

> *the whole world became perfectly silent, and a flight of gulls crossed the sky, first one gull leading, then another, and in this extraordinary silence and peace, in this pallor, in this purity, bells struck eleven times, the sound fading up there among the gulls.*

Birds, says David Bradshaw, "fly above London's social and economic divisions and accentuate the oneness of things". The "essential unanimity" of Londoners is stressed by their collective response to the car which travels from Bond Street to Buckingham Palace and the aeroplane which soars above it while, as Bradshaw says, "the theme of communality is sustained by the novel's dominant narrative technique". Just as Clarissa and Peter Walsh "lived in each other", and Clarissa feels "part of people she had never met", so Woolf thought we could all share the experience of others. Clarissa feels "quite continuously" a sense of the "existence" of friends and acquaintances scattered about west London. Her parties are "an offering; to combine, to create..."

Is this sense of "group consciousness", and in particular Clarissa's identification with Septimus, sentimental? Perhaps. Plenty of critics have seen it as such. It is also at odds with the contrary impression *Mrs Dalloway* gives us – that its characters are trapped in solitary lives, struggling to make sense of the past and come to terms with an uncertain future.

How disturbing is Mrs Dalloway?

For all its brilliance, the party at the end of *Mrs Dalloway* is an anti-climax. Clarissa's anxieties about its success or failure "seem trivial in view of what lies beyond the fairy-lights of her garden", says Elaine Showalter. A reading of the novel which celebrates Clarissa as an artist whose medium is parties "does not seem justified". As Woolf takes us into the minds of the guests, "we see that their facades of festivity and good breeding conceal a terror of ageing and death". Coming together is a way of affirming continuity – of affirming life. Sally and Peter find the party an opportunity to remind themselves they are still capable of passion; for old Mrs Hilbery, the laughter is a way of forgetting that "it is certain we must die".

Woolf's satire is at her sharpest in describing the party – everyone at it, including Clarissa, seems ridiculous. Throughout the novel Peter has judged her most harshly. He has no patience with her in her role as "perfect hostess":

Here's she been, all the time I've been in India; mending her dress; playing about; going to parties.

He attacks her worldliness, her coldness, her "timid; hard; arrogant; prudish" manner, her conventionality, her bowing to Richard Dalloway's view of the world:

The public-spirited, British Empire, tariff-reform, governing-class spirit... With twice his wits, she had to see things through his eyes.

Although our view of Peter and Doris Kilman is very different, their attacks on Clarissa have something in common. Miss Kilman attacks Clarissa from motives of hatred and jealousy, Peter from frustrated love and admiration; the grounds of the attack, however – Clarissa's useless, luxurious existence, her "delicate body, her air of freshness and fashion" – are similar. The criticisms are borne out by Clarissa's tendency to be frivolous, as when she says of her dresses that "You could wear them at Hatfield; at Buckingham Palace. She had worn them at Hatfield; at

Buckingham Palace"; or when she considers that by loving her roses she is helping "the Albanians, or was it the Armenians?" At these points we are invited, says Hermione Lee, "to direct against her the kind of hostility felt by Doris Kilman, or, at least, the kind of satire expressed by Peter Walsh".

At the party, which reflects all Woolf's fascinated dislike for the world of society hostesses, Clarissa's sympathy for Septimus is set sharply against the "corruption, lies, chatter" of

---

PARTIES

According to her husband, Leonard, "the idea of a party" always excited Virginia Woolf, "and in practice she was very sensitive to the actual mental and physical excitement of the party itself, the rise of temperature of mind and body, the ferment and fount of noise". In a recent biography, Alexandra Harris says she used to think of parties as both glamorous and grotesque. "She would protest about having to waste time at these parties but there was always, too, something in them that she found alluring. She recorded their rituals with fascination, and she grasped the point of superficiality... She saw the composed party as a kind of art."

In "Portrait of the Artist as Middle-Aged Woman", Jacob Littlejohn says the "heightened view of existence" Clarissa experiences at parties is reminiscent of that other iconic party giver of 20th century literature, Scott Fitzgerald's Jay Gatsby. "What she liked was simply life," reflects Peter, when considering Clarissa's reason for enjoying parties ∎

her life. The party, says Lee, "emphasizes the ironic dichotomy between youthful aspirations and middle-aged resignation". This shows most startlingly in the appearance of Sally Seton, no wild young thing any longer but a complacent Mancunian housewife. Sally and Peter compare their past hopes with what they've actually achieved. "'Have you written?' she asked him... 'Not a word!'" Lady Bruton observes that Richard has lost his chance of a seat in the Cabinet. They are all seen as failures in a system of which Septimus Smith has been the victim. The Prime Minister is insignificant. Lady Bradshaw is "a sea lion on the edge of its tank, barking for invitations".

The way the party starts downstairs, in the servants' quarters, says Lee,

> sets it in its full triviality against the world of the "lower classes" which Virginia Woolf (though never very realistically) likes to use as a contrast to the world of the "gentry"... Thus Clarissa's "offering", her "triumph", her attempt to "kindle and illuminate", on which the book converges, are seen as hollow, trivial and corrupt, providing satisfaction for the least satisfactory part of her character.

At the party we see Clarissa both at her best, when she retreats to think about Septimus, and at her worst. First we are given a number of external views of her. Ellie Henderson guesses that Clarissa "had not meant to ask her this year"; Sir Harry, the Academician, likes her "in spite of her damnable, difficult, upper-class refinement, which made it impossible to ask Clarissa Dalloway to sit on his knee". Jim Hutton, the young intellectual, thinks her "a prig. But how charming to look at!"

The way different people see Clarissa reflects Woolf's view of the shadowy, unfixed nature of personality. In "The Russian Point of View" Woolf talks of the "streaked, involved, inextricably confused" nature of existence – what we see of others is determined by our own perspective and limitations. As Valentine Cunningham observes, our failure to know much about ourselves and others is a failure "the novel endorses widely". Septimus is wholly uncertain of his identity. Clarissa "would not say of herself, I am this, I am that." The failure is dramatised in what Cunningham calls a "stammering" over naming, especially at the party.

"Who is this?" Sally asks as she arrives. Peter knows: it's old Mrs Hilbery. But he doesn't know "that lady standing by the curtain... Davidson, was that her name?" Many of those thronging to the party get named at the door by Mr Wilkins, who is employed to name them, though, says Cunningham,

he seems only to know them by titles, Lady and Miss this, Sir John and Lady that... But who, familiarly titled or not, are Betty Whatshername, Ameilia Whatsername, Sir Somebody Something, So-and-So, and all the vaguely named rest? The novel's play of remembering, knowing and naming keeps lapsing, tragically, even tragi-comically, like this, into forgetting, not knowing, misnaming, or not being able to name at all.

This vagueness is like a "kind of counter rhetoric" to what Cunningham calls the novel's "wonderful radical thinginess", the stress on hats, dresses, kitchen utensils, etc. The writing keeps aggressively "pointing at what it and its people want us to see and know... There, it keeps saying, there she was, there he was, there were the roses." This rhetorical device is called deixis – the use of demonstratives, adverbs of place, pronouns and

Mrs Dalloway's party, a lithograph

definite articles. They mount up, these deictic ('pointing', as with an imaginary index finger) efforts: this, here, that, these, she, he, it, there, there, there, all, says Cunningham, "striving to fix moments, persons, things, to place them precisely". But often it's not clear what is being pointed at, in particular who it is pronouns are actually referring to. "These confident pointings just won't sustain the examination they provoke as to the nature of the real presence they claim." So when Clarissa walks through London and we are told that "loving it as she did with an absurd and faithful passion, being part of it" we're not at all clear what the "it" refers to: London? The world of shops and shopkeepers? Life? As often in the novel, it's not clear.

There is no real certainty, says Cunningham, and

little defence against madness and death in any solid world of things made really present and reliably knowable. All the novel's insistence and forcefully declarative thisness and thereness will in fact be as fragile as any of its patently false visions and dubious revelations. Things cannot be relied on. Indeed, though the lovely trivia of the world may indeed be felt as blessings, they also present real dementing horrors, as troubling agents of death and annihilation. The gentlest people are armed with pen-knives and scissors and needles. The ordinary is deeply hurtful.

Impressions *raze*, *graze*, *concuss*, *scrape*, *cut*. Clocks *shred* and *slice* time.

London is full of June sunshine but it is also threatening. Septimus stands helplessly watching:

In the street vans roared past him; brutality blared out on placards; women burnt alive; and once a maimed file of lunatics being exercised or displayed for the diversion of the populace (who laughed aloud) ambled and nodded and grinned past him...

Clarissa thinks Mr William Willett's daylight saving scheme – putting the clocks back to make the summer evenings last longer – is a "revolution" putting time and death in their place, signalling a triumph for the life of London.* But in the very same passage the city's refusal to give in to darkness is rendered in a death-reminding metaphor. London "rushed her bayonets into the sky, pinned her [the evening], constrained her to partnership in her revelry". The language reminds us, in what Cunningham calls "one of the novel's more horrific ironies of timing", that Septimus has just bayonetted himself on the spiked iron railings. "Through him, blundering, bruising, went the rusty spikes," thinks Clarissa when she hears of it. The vision of London as both blessed and full of

* The scheme had been adopted a few years earlier, in 1916.

death is there from the third paragraph of *Mrs Dalloway*. "What a lark!" Clarissa thinks, but also: "What a plunge!"

If London can seem an earthly paradise, says Cunningham, "it is just as much, or more, a Purgatorio, an Inferno even". "Horror! Horror!"

POLITICS IN JUNE 1923

On 22 May, a couple of weeks before the day of *Mrs Dalloway*, the Conservative Prime Minister, Bonar Law, retired on grounds of health – he died a few months later, of throat cancer – to be succeeded first by Stanley Baldwin, then, a few months later, by Ramsay MacDonald, the country's first Labour PM. It is the fastest turnover of prime ministers in British political history. The Tory party was in turmoil, which led to the formation of the 1922 Committee, whose mission was to preserve "true", traditional Conservatism. It ended the coalition with the Liberals, who went into the wilderness from which they have never returned.

To this day, ministers of Conservative administrations are answerable to the Committee. Socially the country itself was convulsed: in 1926, with the General Strike, it would result in the closest Britain would come to civil war, or revolution, since the 17th century.

The Woolfs were socialists, openly so. In 1920 Leonard agreed to stand as Labour candidate for one of the University parliamentary seats which then existed. He published polemical articles and books advocating socialist reform. Virginia often accompanied him to political meetings. They were both members of the Fabian Society ■

Rezia Smith "wanted to cry" – as Kurtz does in Conrad's *Heart of Darkness*. J. Hillis Miller thinks a novel, for Woolf, "is the place of death made visible". His fellow American critic, Harold Bloom, says it is difficult to defend *Mrs Dalloway* "from moral judgements that call Woolf's stance wholly nihilistic".

For all its half-consoling notion of "group consciousness", the novel holds no ultimate promise of society being radically transformed, though its values are changing. As Elizabeth Abel notes, Elizabeth's relationship with the grasping Miss Kilman is the modern counterpart of Clarissa's love for Sally Seton. Miss Kilman's possessive desire for Elizabeth parodies the Shakespearian lines used about that love. "If it were now to die, 'twere now to be most happy" becomes "If she [Miss Kilman] could grasp her, if she could make her hers absolutely, and forever and then die; that was all she wanted." Sally walked with Clarissa on the terrace on Bourton; Miss Kilman takes Elizabeth to the Army and Navy Stores – a busy shop in place of a cosy female sanctuary.

There are compensations for Elizabeth. She will have a profession. She may have a more active role in society, though her dreams are vague and we can't be sure. "If [Woolf] surrounds the past with an aureole, she points to the future in silence," says Abel.

The ending of *Mrs Dalloway* is not altogether bleak. Richard Dalloway may be too shy to tell his wife he loves her, yet he notices how beautiful his daughter is and can't stop telling her so. The power of feeling doesn't disappear as we grow older, Peter says, and Sally agrees: "she felt more deeply, more passionately, every year". Richard has "improved" with age, observes Sally as she leaves the party, adding: "What does the brain matter... compared with the heart?" And Peter wonders what fills him with "extraordinary excitement" and realises it is Clarissa.

Mrs Dalloway ends with a typical deictic gesture: "For there she was". We must take Woolf's heroine as we find her, as indeed we must take ourselves. She has lost her youth, yet she has retained some of its spirit; she still fills Peter with excitement and even "terror"; and while her identification with Septimus may be sentimental it is part of her coming to terms with the inevitable limitations of middle age. The novel creates a world which is shadowy and disturbing but it is not, perhaps, as nihilistic as Harold Bloom suggests, ending, as it begins, with a sense of new possibilities – perhaps even, as Elaine Showalter has it, "with a tribute to endurance, survival and joy".

CRITICS ON *MRS DALLOWAY*

"Do her characters live?... I feel that they do live, but not continuously, whereas the characters of Tolstoy (let us say) live continuously."
E.M. Forster, 1926

"Woolf's snobbery, preciousness and bonkersness come through on every page [of her novels]. She has benefited immensely from a gang of sycophants in the literary trade and academia talking her up for nearly a century, not so much for her own sake as for the sake of the cult of Bloomsbury that she incarnated so well."
Simon Heffer, *The Daily Telegraph*, 9th January 2010

"There is no reason to suppose Mrs Woolf would know which end of the cradle to stir."
Q.D. Leavis (who resented her privileged upbringing), 1938

Virginia Woolf *"is an English novelist of manners writing village gossip about a village called Bloomsbury"*.
Hugh Kenner, 1984

"Bloomsbury were serious but not serious in the overwhelming style of such acquaintances as Sidney and Beatrice Webb (Fabian socialists prepared to have their heads turned by Stalin). They believed in laughter. (Laughter, in all its registers, from cruel to merry, resounds in Woolf's work, not least in her diary and letters.)"
Andrew McNeillie, 2000

CHRONOLOGY

1882 Virginia Woolf born, to Leslie Stephen (founder of the *Dictionary of National Biography*) and Julia Duckworth. James Joyce also born. Darwin and Trollope die.

1885 Virginia's mother dies. "This brought on my first breakdown," she later recorded.

1901 Queen Victoria dies.

1904 Leslie Stephen dies, causing a second breakdown.

1907 Writes her first novel, "Melymbrosia", working title for *The Voyage Out*.

1909 Lytton Strachey proposes marriage.

1910 Edward VII dies. So does Tolstoy. George V becomes King. Roger Fry's Post-Impressionist Exhibition.

1912 Marries Leonard Woolf. Honeymoon in Provence, Spain and Italy.

1913 Suicide attempt in March. Remains under care of nurses and husband for rest of the year.

1914 4th August, First World War begins. James Joyce's *The Dubliners*.

1915 *The Voyage Out*

1917 Founds The Hogarth Press with her husband.

1919 Buys Monk's House, Rodmell, Sussex.

1922 First meets Vita Sackville-West. T.S. Eliot's *The Waste Land*.

1923 Working on "The Hours", which becomes *Mrs Dalloway*. Katherine Mansfield dies.

1924 Lenin, Conrad and Kafka die. Ramsay MacDonald becomes Prime Minister. The Woolfs buy the lease of 52 Tavistock Square in London.

1925 *Mrs Dalloway*

1927 *To the Lighthouse*

1928 *Orlando*. Series of lectures in Cambridge on which she bases *A Room of One's Own*.

1931 *The Waves*

1939 Second World War begins. The Woolfs – he Jewish, both left-wing – were prominent on Gestapo death lists. Both had made suicide plans.

1941 March 28th, fearing permanent madness, goes to the River Ouse, near Monk's House. Loads her pockets with stones and drowns herself.

FURTHER READING

Abel, Elizabeth, *Virginia Woolf and the Fictions of Psychoanalysis*, University of Chicago Press, 1989

Bloom, Harold (ed.), *Virginia Woolf: Modern Critical Views*, Chelsea House Publishers (NY), 1986

Bloom, Harold (ed.), *Virginia Woolf's Mrs Dalloway: Modern Critical Interpretations*, Chelsea House Publishers (NY), 1988

Bradshaw, David (introduction), *Mrs Dalloway*, Oxford World's Classics, 2008

Cunningham, Valentine (introduction), *Mrs Dalloway*, Vintage Classics, 2004

Daiches, David, *Virginia Woolf*, New Directions Books (Connecticut), 1942

Daiches, David, *The Novel and the Modern World*, University of Chicago Press, 1960

Daiches, David and Flower, John, *Literary Landscapes*, Bell & Hyman, 1979

Dowling, David, *Mrs Dalloway: Mapping Streams of Consciousness*, Twayne Publishers (Boston), 1991

Hawthorn, Jeremy, *Virginia Woolf's Mrs Dalloway*, Sussex University Press, 1975

Lee, Hermione, *Virginia Woolf*, Vintage, 1997

Lee, Hermione, *The Novels of Virginia Woolf*, Methuen, 1977

Majumdar, Robin and McLaurin, Allen (eds.), *Virginia Woolf, The Critical Heritage*, Routledge & Kegan Paul, 1975

Minow-Pinkney, Makiko, *Virginia Woolf & the Problem of subject*, The Harvester Press, 1987

Novak, Jane, *The razor edge of balance: a Study of Virginia Woolf*, University of Miami Press, 1975

Poresky, Louise, *The Elusive Self: Psyche and Spirit in Virginia Woolf's Novels*, Associated University Presses, 1981

Sellers, Susan (ed.), *The Cambridge Companion to Virginia Woolf*, Cambridge University Press, 2010

Showalter, Elaine (introduction), *Mrs Dalloway*, Penguin Books, 1992

Sprague, Claire (ed.) *Virginia Woolf: A Collection of Critical Essays*, Prentice-Hall, 1971

Warner, Eric (ed.), *Virginia Woolf: a Centenary Perspective*, St Martin's Press (NY), 1984

Whitworth, Michael, *Virginia Woolf*, Oxford World's Classics, 2005

Zwerdling, Alex, *Virginia Woolf and the Real World*, University of California Press, 1986

INDEX

First published in 2014 by
Connell Guides
Artist House
35 Little Russell Street
London WC1A 2HH

10 9 8 7 6 5 4 3 2 1

Picture credits:
p.17 © Lebrecht Music and Arts Photo Library/Alamy
p.25 © CSU Archv/Everett/REX
p.61 © Moviestore Collection/REX
p.77 © Moretimer Rare Book Room, Smith College
p.85 © c.Paramount/Everett/REX
p.115 © This image may be used without prior permission for any
scholarly or educational purpose. "Medals." Photograph. Victorian Web.
Web. 28 Nov 2011. http://www.victorianweb.org/images/medals.gif

A CIP catalogue record for this book is available from the British Library.
ISBN 978–1–907776–26–7

Design © Nathan Burton
Assistant Editors:
Katie Sanderson, Paul Woodward & Pierre Smith Khanna

Printed in Italy by LEGO

www.connellguides.com